Focusing on Practical Spirituality
More Books by Meredith Gould

Desperately Seeking Spirituality:
A Field Guide to Practice
(Liturgical Press)

Staying Sober:
Tips for Working a Twelve Step
Program of Recovery
(Hazelden)

Why Is There a Menorah on the Altar?
Jewish Roots of Christian Worship
(Seabury Books)

Come to the Table:
A Passover Seder for Parish Use
(Plowshares Publishing)

The Catholic Home:
Celebrations and Traditions for Holidays,
Feast Days, and Every Day
(Image/Doubleday)

Deliberate Acts of Kindness

A Field Guide to Service As a Spiritual Practice

New Edition

Meredith Gould

Clear Faith Publishing · Princeton, New Jersey
www.clearfaithpublishing.com

Published by Clear Faith Publishing, LLC
23 Lafayette Road
Princeton, NJ 08540

"The Road Ahead" from *Thoughts in Solitude* by Thomas Merton. Copyright 1958 by the Abbey of Our Lady of Gethsemani. Copyright renewed 1986 by the Trustees of the Thomas Merton Legacy Trust. Reprinted by permission of Farrar, Straus and Giroux, LLC.

Cover Design by Stefan Killen of Red+Company
Interior Design by Doug Cordes

ISBN 978-1-940414-13-3

For those getting ready to shift from standing and waiting,
to actively serving others with grace,
as well as those already doing so.

Contents

Foreword to the New Edition   IX

Foreword to the First Edition   XI

Chapter 1
Service as a Spiritual Practice   1

Chapter 2
Discerning the Call   13

Chapter 3
Discovering Your Place   31

Chapter 4
Becoming and Being Involved   57

Chapter 5
The Shadow Side of Service   75

Afterword to the First Edition
Service Is Its Own Reward   101

Notes   105

Index   111

Foreword to the New Edition

Service to others is a timeless spiritual practice, but books about it occasionally need updating. I realized *Deliberate Acts of Kindness* could do with an update while rereading it to propose yet another book about spiritual life, *Desperately Seeking Spirituality: A Field Guide to Practice* (Liturgical Press, 2016).

I was happy and relieved to discover that although *Deliberate Acts of Kindness* was first published in 2002, much of it remains what publishers call "evergreen." More specifically, introductory narrative for each chapter and Contemplative Writing exercises still make sense in their original form. But I found that quite a few of the practical tips needed updating or flat-out deletion. Plus, some content simply worked better in *Desperately Seeking Spirituality*, where I could (and did) explore it in more detail.

The structure also worked, so I kept it while tweaking some chapter titles. Speaking of which, I recommend reading Chapter 1: Service as a Spiritual Practice and Chapter 2: Discerning the Call in sequence. Feel free to dip in and out of the other chapters. To learn more about why I initially wrote *Deliberate Acts of Kindness*, please read my original preface on page [XI]. Please keep in mind that I wrote it long before the attack of September 11, 2001. Much has happened since then to challenge our nation's kindness and generosity.

But wait, there's (always) more!

The original book didn't have an index to help readers find things. Nor did it have endnotes with links to online resources and commentary (read: stuff I'd say *sotto voce* if you were sitting next to me). This new edition has both an index and endnotes.

Spoiler alert: counsel for doing good, attributed to John Wesley and brought to public secular awareness by U.S. Democrats during the 2016 presidential election, was included in the first edition and retained in this one. You'll find it on page 60.

Oh, why wait? Here it is again:

> "Do all the good you can. By all the means you can.
> In all the ways you can. In all the places you can. At
> all the times you can. To all the people you can. As
> long as ever you can."

I, for one, am hoping for a return to greater kindness and generosity, mercy and justice. Intentionally. Deliberately. And so, I feel compelled to add—and end with—AMDG.*

---

ad majorem Dei gloriam (to the greater glory of God.)

Foreword to the First Edition
(2002)

Running late for an afternoon meeting, I zipped into the parking lot about five...ten... miles over the speed limit. No spaces. Wait, there *was* a space—and a very convenient one, I might add—marked HANDICAPPED. Just as I was about to park, the words "nice values" floated to the surface of my awareness, followed by this kicker, "and you call yourself a Woman of God?"

I didn't take the space. And no, God didn't lead me to one with time on a parking meter. The spot I finally found was a few blocks away. What occurred next was truly remarkable. When I walked back to the parking lot an hour later, I discovered the spot I had coveted was occupied. The car had official HANDICAPPED license plates. In that moment, I was able to see just how solid—and how slippery—my own commitment to human decency can be at times.

What does it take to transform "random acts of kindness" into *deliberate* acts of kindness, compassion, and integrity? What does it take to transform navel-gazing into an awareness of greater purpose? What does it take to move from head to heart? More specifically, what has it taken for me to evolve in these directions just a teensy bit?

My mother comes immediately to mind. Somewhere in Israel is a grove of mature trees with my name on them because she made me buy little leaf-shaped stamps from the Jewish National Fund during the 1960s. Somewhere in a developing country whose name has changed multiple times in the past four decades, at least one person has survived to adulthood because Mommy made me collect pennies for UNICEF instead of candy on Halloween. Today, I have great teeth and eat chocolate whenever I can, but the *habit* of considering others runs deep, thanks, in large part, to her indefatigable efforts. Over the years, other sources and situations have also contributed to being able to hear and heed the call to service.

In 1988, I visited a well-known yoga retreat center and became fairly smitten with the entire scene—Guru included. One year later, as the result of a near-complete emotional and spiritual meltdown, I ditched my fancy job in advertising and PR, as well as the house I salvaged from my first messy marriage, and decided to become part of that community. There, I encountered splendid opportunities to learn how true service is not about the preferences and convenience of the one who serves. There, I observed the dubious value of serving as an act of pure obedience. And I discovered *karma yoga.*

In case you don't already know, *karma yoga* is the path of working one's butt off doing selfless service (*seva*). The spiritual reward for all this labor is the illuminating joy of seeing how your human foibles like resistance, resentment, and sheer laziness block spiritual attainment. While I wasn't enormously thrilled to encounter the shadow side of self—mine or anyone else's—*karma yoga* was clearly the path for me! At last, I'd found an artful, spiritually correct way to camouflage worka-holism. I happily worked myself to death for the promise of a better Self. Indeed, when I left nearly two years later, I did so with a more generous spirit, with slightly less judgment, and all gung-ho about the benefits of selfless service.

As it turned out, I had missed an important lesson along the way, so God and the angels arranged a makeup class that would last another few years.

I got all the stuff about "no light without darkness," "no joy without tears," and "no true life without death." What I'd missed was the sacred and necessary interconnectedness of giving and receiving. It would soon become painfully appar-ent that my reluctance to seek help for myself was stunting my psychospiritual growth.

It's lonely at the bottom. I would discover this the hard way. Nothing less than a total meltdown of body, mind, and spirit would get my full attention. And so it wasn't until stumbling onto the path of twelve-step recovery that I learned how to ask for—and gratefully received—help I sorely needed. Within months of being tenderized, I had my first felt experience of empathy.[1] As I listened to someone else talk about feelings and fears, I noticed my throat constrict with unshed tears. My heart actually physically ached. In that moment, the expression "I feel your pain" shifted from being an annoying bit of psychobabble to being absolute truth. Separation disappeared. Reaching out to another felt exactly like being embraced. I would come to understand how service, a key component of the twelve-step programs of recovery, could be both a powerful antidote to self-absorption and balm to the wounded soul.[2]

Learning when, where, and how to be of service is a process. Sometimes whatever I've learned thus far slips away almost entirely, as it did the afternoon I nearly stole that handicapped parking space. More and more, I wake up just in time to do the Right Thing.

But enough about me; what about you? Why are you being called into service? Why now?

Maybe, having explored a number spiritual traditions and practices, you're hankering to become a more expansive Self. Maybe, thanks to a potent combination of therapy and life experience, you see how other Flesh Units deserve your support. Maybe you hail from a family with a long-standing tradition of philanthropy and you're ready to make your own mark. Maybe, after a stint of court-mandated community service, you feel compelled to do some more on your own. Maybe you've yet to answer call waiting, even though the cosmic beeper resounds deep within.

This book is about how to respond when the call to service cannot be put on hold any longer. It's primarily a guide to hearing the call—then doing something intentional about answering it. You'll find practical tips for deciding where to serve, how to enter a variety of service environments, and strategies for surviving less-than-divine aspects you'll encounter along the way.

I've used a tips format so you won't have to wade through pages of prose before getting to hints that will help you endure the volunteers' meeting this very afternoon. And, because I've come to believe that service itself qualifies as a spiritual practice, each chapter includes at least one "Contemplative

Writing Exercise" I hope you'll dive into, even if the reflection questions make you feel uneasy. Please consider dedicating a special journal to the cause of discovering a cause. Or don't. In any event, I hope you find this book a useful and enjoyable way to either enter or restore your commitment to service. May you be blessed by all your efforts to serve others.

CHAPTER I

Service as a Spiritual Practice

INTRODUCTION

Our spiritual forebears knew there was something special about feeding the hungry, helping the poor, welcoming the stranger, and lifting up the brokenhearted.[3] Considering that daily survival—without indoor plumbing, no less—was an all-consuming enterprise for just about everyone, their insistence that selflessness represented the fullest expression of spiritual life was truly radical.

Throughout religious history, prophets in every tradition have made a fuss about the heavenly virtues of making nice. The fact that several died trying to make this point may explain why lesser mortals have failed to fully appreciate the spiritual benefit of righteousness in the form of generosity. To this very day, proponents of the major world religions view service as spirit-in-action and, if not a direct means of salvation, at least a way of doing quality time while here on earth.

If the mere mention of world religions—any or all them—gags you, try to remember that for every spiritually-oriented person who recoils with horror from the formalism of organized religion, there is a religious one who squints suspiciously at what-all is currently classified as spiritual.[4] Try not to get too distracted by disputes about form and expression. Instead, focus on the one thing major world religions agree upon in either Scripture or commentary: the importance of serving others with decency, generosity, and love. Here's a closer look at what Western traditions say about service, especially its impact on the hereafter.

JUDAISM

For observant Jews, the practice of righteousness (*tzedakah*) is much more than a decent thing to do; it's a commandment (*mitzvah*). While not one of the tabled top ten, it's among 613 individual commandments forming Jewish law (*Halakhah*). The twelfth-century philosopher Moses Maimonides identified *tzedakah* as perhaps the most important obligation of Jewish life—a pretty awesome designation when you consider the complexity of *Halakhah*.

Flip through the first five books of the Bible for detailed instructions about what a righteous person ought to do and what will happen when guidelines are either followed or ignored. In Genesis, for example, Abraham and Sarah welcome three strangers and, as is frequently the case, the visitors turn out to be angels (Gn 18). The aged Sarah is blessed with fertility, Isaac is born, and a nation is founded (Gn 21:1-22:18).

In Leviticus and Deuteronomy, God commands Moses to teach the Israelites about such things as the practice of tithing (i.e., giving one-tenth of one's income), leaving the gleanings of harvest for the poor and alien, and giving generously to those in need without a grudging heart (e.g., Lv 27:30-33; Dt 26:12-13). Obedience to these commandments, the ancient Israelites are told, will bring peace and prosperity; disobedience is sure to bring sudden terror, wasting diseases, desolation, and plagues.

While Jewish response to strict observance has changed over the centuries, *tzedakah* has retained importance as a value and form of ethical action going far beyond donating money, planting trees in Israel, or sending a stranger home from the Passover table with leftovers in plastic containers they may keep. These are necessary but not sufficient acts. For Jews, generosity is a way of being and being-in-the-world that includes a passion for social justice.

As the "chosen people of God," in addition to being survivors of slavery and genocide, Jews throughout history and of every movement have embraced the moral responsibility to further human rights and freedom.[5] Recognizing that all beings are created in the likeness and image of God (Gn 1:26) is reason enough to extend loving-kindness to all God's created. Righteousness and identity are therefore bound together in this lifetime.

Depending on the era, rabbinic sage, and God-only-knows what else, Jewish belief is not exactly divided, but not exactly coherent about what happens after death and why. Rabbis of the Talmudic era taught that adherence to *mitzvot* would be reported after death but should, because they're divinely decreed, be followed without that spiritual carrot.

First-century rabbis had a heaven (*Gan Eden*) and hell (*Gehinnom*) thing figured out, complete with time frames for arrival and departure from each. By the time Maimonides got around to tidying up centuries of written and spoken stuff, heaven and hell had been reduced or, depending on your perspective, elevated to metaphor. In any event, Maimonides considered intellectual achievement as valid a qualification for immortality as moral action.

Judaism also had mystics who spent considerable time and energy arguing about whether the transmigration of souls was a form of punishment for committed sins (i.e., not following *mitzvot*) or just a cosmic second chance to do a better job of bringing righteousness into the world.

If Judaism makes anything clear, it's that serving others is more than good; it's essential, and you'll have to wait to see how eternal consequences of social action pan out. With 613 commandments to follow, don't count on *tzedakah* clinching your entrance into the heavenly Garden of Eden (if it exists). On the other hand, it can't hurt. Add prayer and repentance to the mix, and you're almost there.

CONTEMPLATIVE WRITING EXERCISE
TZEDAKAH

Moses Maimonides, who took on the humongous task of collecting and compiling all extant Jewish oral traditions, legal practices, rituals, and customs, in addition to centuries of rabbinic commentaries, debates, and rulings, into a ginormous encyclopedia, made pithy observations about the Jewish practice of *tzedakah*. According to him, the Eight Degrees of Righteousness in the form of giving proceeds incrementally. Not only does each stage represent a deeper level of consciousness about the act of giving but also a more comprehensive understanding about the impact of receiving.

MAIMONIDES' EIGHT DEGREES OF TZEDAKAH

1. To give grudgingly, reluctantly, or with regret;
2. To give less than one should, but with grace;
3. To give what one should, but only after being asked;
4. To give before one is asked;
5. To give without knowing who will receive it, although the recipient knows the identity of the giver;
6. To give without making known one's identity;
7. To give so that neither giver nor receiver knows the identity of the others;
8. To help another to become self-supporting, by means of a gift, a loan, or by finding employment for the one in need.

When it comes to why and how people give, apparently not much has changed in almost 1000 years. As you contemplate this enduring wisdom, write your gut responses to these questions:

- Where am I right now in relation to the standards of giving?
- Under what circumstances do I adjust the way I give to others?
- What would it take for me to consistently achieve the highest level of *tzedakah*?

CHRISTIANITY

Christianity's scriptural basis for social action is manifest most notably in Jesus the Christ's teaching about the greatest commandment. When quizzed on the subject by hostile Pharisees. Jesus selected the commandment to "love your neighbor as yourself" from the hefty list in Leviticus. He likened what would become known as the Golden Rule to the first and greatest commandment to "love the Lord, your God, with all your heart, with all your soul, and with all your mind" (Mt 22: 37–38), thus placing love at the center of all Jewish law. Like other rabbis of his time, Jesus advanced the spiritual necessity of hospitality, charitable acts of giving, tithing, and gleaning.

But Jesus, in his role as radical rabbi, had a more expansive notion of *tzedakah*, calling upon followers to surpass the righteousness of dominant priests and teachers of the law. Jesus challenged man-made laws about time, place, person, and manner. All four Gospel books of Christian Scripture present parables and report instances of gleaning, feeding, forgiving, and miraculous healing unfettered by legalistic interpretations about Sabbath observance or who should be worthy of compassion.[6] Mosaic law may have gone on and on about the importance of righteous acts, but Jesus actually hung out with lepers and other outcasts—sometimes without ritually washing!

Actually, Jesus did more than hang out with the dregs of ancient society; he reached out to them and defended their God-given right to existence. The Kingdom of Heaven truly awaits those who serve the less savory members of the human family. There's no debate among Christians about whether heaven and hell exist—they do. Nor is there debate about who gets a trip to eternal paradise—believers. Things heat up among the faithful over the role "good works" play, relative to salvation.

"Faith by itself, if it is not accompanied by action, is dead," wrote James in an epistle to members of the early Church (Jas 2:14-18). Nevertheless, this passage juxtaposed with others, most notably those by the apostle Paul, about the supervening power of grace through faith in the life (e.g., 2 Cor 12:9), death, and Resurrection of Jesus have resulted in centuries of denominational wrangling and no shortage of bloodied battles among Christians. Indeed, scholars have argued the Protestant Reformation happened in large part because of Luther's scripturally based insistence that grace, not greasing the local cleric's palm, was the sole source of salvation. In recent years, Catholics and Lutherans have formally agreed that salvation is obtained through the merciful grace of God, although most Catholics would still insist, albeit more quietly, that the willingness and ability to perform goods works is itself *prima facie* evidence of grace.[7]

Sectarianism aside, Christians of all denominations share with Jews a deep and abiding regard for righteous action, which, for Christians especially, is perceived as a form of love-in-action. Both crucifix and cross express this love, the former as evidence of obedience and sacrifice for others; the latter as evidence of a God who is eternal, living, and present at all times. Christians also share with Jews a call to address the root causes of human suffering.

CONTEMPLATIVE WRITING EXERCISE
THE RULE OF ST. BENEDICT

During the sixth century, Benedict of Nursia wrote the definitive handbook for Christian monasticism, which, by the time he took up the quill, had already been plodding along for 200 years. The Rule is relatively brief yet comprehensive, providing excruciatingly detailed directions for living spiritual life in community. St. Benedict covered everything from the sublime (e.g., how to integrate prayer into daily life) to the ridiculous (e.g., how monks should sleep). With specific regard to service, Chapter 4 lists no fewer than seventy-four "tools of good works," and in Chapter 53, "The Reception of Guests," readers are reminded that "all who arrive as guests are to be welcomed like Christ."

Despite archaic language, the Rule has enduring meaning and value.[8] Taken as a whole, the rule outlines a way of life based on order, discipline, and balance. The stability resulting from the spiritual lifestyle, insists St. Benedict, is what makes it possible to successfully integrate work-in-the-world with the work-of-God.

The Rule of St. Benedict, which has survived for nearly 1500 years, also has value for those living in the secular world. Write your spontaneous responses to these questions:

- How do I currently balance interior and exterior needs and responsibilities?
- Under what circumstances or conditions am I willing to be humble, honest, and obedient?
- What would it take for me to be able to see God in all people?

THE EASTERN TRADITIONS

While it may seem overly simplistic to lump Buddhism with the conglomeration of sects constituting Hinduism, both have similar perspectives about service. Indeed, the whole point to serving others shifts somewhat when it comes to these Eastern faith traditions, primarily because of their responses to two cosmic questions.

Ask "Why am I here?" and get ready to wrap your brain around the concept of "Full Realization" or "Enlightenment" which, by the way, is the liberating bliss of realizing everything is illusion. The point of being *here* is to get to *there*, and serving others provides a means of transportation. Ask "What happens when I die?" and you can expect to hear something that sounds like, "plan on coming back until you get it right." The doctrine of reincarnation guarantees eternal *lives*, and service is one way to get it "right."

The principle of *quid pro quo*, embedded in the Judeo-Christian Golden Rule, is more blatantly revealed and revered by Eastern practitioners who believe true service is, at its core, an active self-purification for the giver. Ethical and compassionate action not only provides opportunities to reduce the personal greed, selfishness, and cravings inhibiting spiritual progress, but it also gives rise to the merit (*punna*) which, in turn, purifies the mind of ideas, beliefs, and attitudes causing suffering (*dukkha*). The Buddhist practice of charity (*dana*) and Hindu practice of selfless service (*seva*) plus the wisdom emerging with regular meditation is what makes Enlightenment (*nirvana*) possible.

Although Eastern practitioners are more apt to call them "dialogues," sectarian squabbles about social responsibility exist here as well because...humans. Mahayana and Theravada Buddhists, for example, are divided about whether liberation should be put on hold for the sake of others.

Mahayana Buddhists venerate the *bodhisattva,* a being who practices generosity, morality, renunciation, patience, truthfulness determination, loving-kindness, and even-mindedness throughout many lives to lessen the *dukkha* of others. The *bodhisattva* voluntarily stalls final attainment (and therefore release from the painful cycle of life, death, and rebirth) to lead other sentient beings to *nirvana.* By serving others first, the *bodhisattva* represents the ultimate expression of compassion.

Theravada Buddhists invite all sentient beings to reduce their *own* suffering by seeking release from greed, selfishness, acquisitiveness, and attachment through practices (including ethical actions) that expose and expunge negative mental states. There is nothing to hold onto; letting go and giving it all away is a path to and beyond Self.

In the Eastern traditions, meditation and its many forms is a core practice, one revealing the ego's desires and the mind's frantic attempts to cover them up. Practiced regularly and diligently, meditation brings freedom from the ignorance giving rise to *dukkha* and softens the heart so the supreme Oneness of all beings is realized—if only for a split second of ecstatic consciousness in this lifetime. (Maybe longer in the next, depending on your level of attainment.)

CONTEMPLATIVE WRITING EXERCISE
METTA MEDITATION

Despite any appearances to the contrary, meditation offers a way to become free from the individual self and its narcissistic concerns and petty problems. Compassion, the ability to act in response to another's suffering, is a quality-of-being that can be cultivated. Loving-kindness (*metta*) meditation is an exquisite practice to help open mind and heart to others.

The practice of *metta* dissolves fear and anxiety through the silent or quietly audible repetition of four short resolves or wishes, starting with your own beleaguered self:

> *May I be free from danger.*
> *May I have mental happiness.*
> *May I have physical happiness.*
> *May I have the ease of well-being.*

Next, your loving wishes for freedom and safety are gradually extended to categories of others both known and unknown, liked and disliked. This may be specific, like "May my sister Louise be free from danger" or "May the bozo who took the last donut at the meeting have mental happiness."[9] Or you can extend *metta* to general categories, like "May all first responders be free from danger," invoking larger and more inclusive categories until you're able to end with:

> *May all beings without exception be free from danger.*
> *May all beings without exception have mental happiness.*
> *May all beings without exception have physical happiness.*
> *May all beings without exception have ease of well-being.*

Try meditating this way when you first wake up and before drifting off to sleep at night so it becomes part of you, a quality-of-being that resonates even when you're stuck in traffic—or life. Metta meditation will serve you well as you answer the call to service.

CHAPTER 2

Discerning the Call

INTRODUCTION

You've been traipsing along a spiritual path for a while; now what? At the beginning of your quest for an authentic life, it was enough to ponder your own fascinating existence. Big questions took up a lot of psychic space: "Is there a God?" "Who am I?" "What's all this fuzz doing in my belly button?"

Searching for a means to answer these questions has also occupied huge chunks of time. You've spent countless hours exploring a variety of spiritual practices, searching for the tried-and-true form of prayer or meditation to bring you into closer contact with the Almighty.[10] And although you may have prayed or meditated in the company of like-hearted others, your journey has felt intensely private and personal.

Recently, however, you've noticed a change in how you feel and what you're seeking. You've settled into a more-or-less regular spiritual practice and are on superb speaking terms with God. Yet, a certain restlessness has emerged, one that feels different from the soulless hunger first prompting your spiritual journey. Big questions are getting bigger: "Why am I here?" "What am I called to do?" Other people—their needs, suffering, and sorrows—are becoming ever more alluring. In fact, you're beginning to suspect "it" isn't even about you.

Surprise! What you may have thought was a detour along the spiritual path is really an important destination. You're realizing how spiritual life is ultimately about understanding and acting upon the knowledge that all beings share a sacred heritage.

What you're experiencing is the inexorable pull toward service. Time to accelerate—or celebrate—your growth by reaching out to others, *whether or not they, too, are seeking God.*

More questions loom large: "How do I know that I'm being called?" "How can I serve?" This is stuff you'll need to sort out before you can truly and fully enter into service. The process of noodling around with these questions is a holy endeavor known as "discernment." Tips in this chapter suggest ways of safely diving into this process so you can discover not only whether the incoming call is for you but whether it's even coming from a divine source.

CHAPTER TIPS

Remember that you do not have to be perfect to help others. You just need willingness, humility, and empathy—all of which are difficult enough to cultivate without aiming for perfection as well.

Seek help to figure out how you might be of service. Ask your most perceptive (and honest) friends to describe your best talents, skills, and gifts. Muster the guts to ask if they would gently point out what might graciously be characterized as "areas for improvement" in your temperament and behavior. Better yet, ask them to send you a note or an email about this so you have something tangible to read, save, and ponder over time.

Clear the way for more subtle levels of awareness to emerge. List what you think are wonderfully perfect ways for you to serve, letting reason and logic dictate your choices. Now set this list aside and pursue nothing until after you engage in an inquiry that's guided by Spirit rather than your mind—and possibly your need for recognition.

Here's a good question to ask yourself: "What sort of person would I like to become?"

> *"Fill yourselves first and then only will you be able to give to others."*
> —St. Augustine—

YOU'RE READY TO SERVE OTHERS WHEN...

For some the call to service comes through loud and clear. Then there are those for whom the call to service sounds like unintelligible mumbling, albeit at the soul level. Here are ways to figure out when you're ready to respond to

Divine nagging:
- Suddenly you're seized with an uncontrollable urge to throw extra change into checkout line donation boxes; adopt a child for just pennies a day; participate in blood drives; and donate contents of your pantry (and not the stuff you won't ever eat) to the local food bank.
- Instead of feeling irritated by other people's tales of woe, which heretofore you thought never quite measured up to yours, you start feeling what can only be described as tender empathy.
- After years of tootling around just fine, or close to it, you feel as if something is seriously missing in your life—and you suspect getting a new job, spouse, or zippy red car won't fill the void.
- Having maxed out on psychotherapy, weekend workshops, and self-help books, you've caught yourself wondering how to be useful to others.

There's a lot to be said for the role service plays in reducing self-absorption. Take, for example, the way twelve-step programs of recovery are structured. Here, providing service to others (e.g., "still suffering alcoholics and addicts") is considered a key component. Still, you might want to clean up your act somewhat before submerging yourself in service, so take time to focus on healing your addictions, compulsions, and character disorders—if you have any, of course.

PSYCHOSOCIAL FOUNDATIONS FOR SERVICE

Twentieth-century psychologist Abraham Maslow created a model for human motivation based on a hierarchy of needs. His model is based on five levels of human needs, ranging from basic to esoteric. The epitome of growth, which he termed "self-actualization" cannot be achieved until higher-order psychological needs are fulfilled.

Throughout human history, people have heard and answered the call to service under significantly less-than-optimal conditions, such as war, famine, and stock market crashes. Nevertheless, Maslow's Hierarchy of Needs is useful for understanding what you may need to handle in your personal life before being optimally able to serve others.

MASLOW'S HIERARCHY OF NEEDS

Level I: Physiological Needs
air, water, food, clothing, shelter, sleep, sex

Level II: Safety and Security Needs
order, stability, certainty, routine, familiarity, protection from fear and disease, physical safety, economic security, freedom from threat

Level III: Social Needs
love, acceptance, belonging, affection

Level IV: Esteem Needs
respect and recognition from others, self-respect, sense of prestige

Level V: Self-Actualization Needs
"peak" experiences, fulfilling a sense of Self and calling, opportunities for learning and creating at higher levels

Don't be shy about including requests for divine guidance in your prayers. This is especially helpful if you believe in a Higher Power with a grand plan for your life—not like a puppeteer but a beloved friend with your best interest at heart. Your prayer can be simple, as in: "God, how shall I be of service?" Or it can be more elaborate, as in: "God, I have the opportunity to take on a service commitment that will require lots of energy. Is the timing right for this?"

Feeling antsy, curious, or hankering to do or be something different? If this feeling persists in the face of a life that seems to be otherwise working well, consider that you may be getting called into service.

DISCERNING SERVICE
THE ULTIMATE PRAYER

Grant us ears to hear,
Eyes to see,
Wills to obey,
Hearts to love;
Then declare what you will,
Reveal what you will,
Command what you will,
Demand what you will.

—*Christina Rossetti*

Forget about calling the Psychic Hotline, and use a prayer of
petition to dial direct for the spiritual gift of discernment.
You can keep the supplication short and sweet: "God, I pray
for the knowledge of your will." You can leave it at that and
see what happens. Sooner or later, you'll find yourself getting
marching orders that either don't make sense or you flat out
don't like. At this point, you may want to launch another
little request through prayer: "God, how about giving me the
humility, strength, courage, and willingness to do your will?"
(Don't forget to pray "thank you" when your prayers are
answered—even if you don't like *how* they've been answered.)

A call doesn't happen once and for all. In fact, your call may
be recalled! Keep praying and listening, especially when
something doesn't immediately make sense.

Pay attention when the same message is delivered through
multiple messengers. Maybe you don't think the time is right
to become more active in your community, but isn't it inter-
esting how numerous and diverse invitations to participate
keep showing up?

Got trust issues? These may need attention before you're
able to trust a call to service. Basically, if you believe humans
generally can't be counted on, you're bound to have a bit of
trouble with anything numinous. Perhaps some psychological
digging through therapy is in order. Or participate in a

workshop where you have to do a "trust fall" into the arms of fellow participants.[11] Want to know what trust actually looks like? Spend some time baby watching—humans, kittens, puppies, birds. See how relaxed and open they are to the world around them?

> *"God wants the heart."*
> —The Talmud—

Start noticing when things happen simultaneously. At the oddest times. For no apparent reason. You were thinking wistfully about your former teaching career when someone asked "out of the blue" if you'd lead a workshop. You couldn't resist buying forty-eight rolls of toilet paper on sale, two weeks before the local food pantry "suddenly" put out an emergency request for paper products. Just maybe the so-called coincidences are the invisible hand of God being made visible. Get used to zooming in for a closer look-see whenever you catch yourself thinking:

- "Now, that's strange."
- "What luck!"
- "I never noticed that before."
- "How weird."

Add premonitions to your list of nonmaterial, non-rational clues worth noting. Follow up on your sense of something tugging at your awareness by stopping for a quick confab with the Almighty about where it may be leading. Intuition is developed by paying attention to hunches, no matter how wacky they may seem. Keep a small notepad or index cards on hand, or use your smartphone to send yourself memos or otherwise make note of these flashes of inspiration. Be sure to add the date of your insights. At some future point, maybe years down the line, you'll be amazed at how the dots get connected.[12]

How will you know your call to service is indeed the will of God and not merely something your ego deeply desires? Well, an authentic call will probably have any or all of the following paradoxical characteristics: it will be something that:

- you'd never think of on your own;
- makes total sense given who you are;
- stretches you in body, mind, and spirit;
- invites you to grow where you're already planted.

Another paradox: Have a vision *and* be equally willing to let that vision go. Can't or *won't* let it go? Try loosening your mental grip by shifting the way you think about how and where to serve. Think "whatever" instead of "gotta," "wherever" instead of "there." The knowledge that God will lead you to something much better than you could dream up comes with believing in a loving, wise, merciful God.

Create a "discernment group" or "wisdom circle" organized around exploring the call to service as a spiritual practice. You can accomplish this by gathering a group that:

- involves at least three, but no more than five people;
- meets regularly for at least two, but no more than four hours;
- focuses on the discernment needs of one member at a time;
- makes a commitment to supporting clarity by listening carefully, asking great questions, allowing for silence, and letting Spirit guide the flow;
- understands the importance of intra-group accountability, truthfulness, and shared faith.

Not only is this type of group helpful during the initial process of discerning dharma, vocation, or calling, but it can provide valuable support as issues emerge during the course of serving. If you don't want to create such a group, join one that already exists. If groups give you the creeps, sign on with a spiritual advisor who will work with you directly.[13]

To make sure you're on the right path, measure the integrity of your call against universal spiritual values. Are you being called to serve in a way that furthers truth, justice, tolerance, kindness, compassion, and so forth? This examination of conscience is especially important if you've been known to spiritualize events (e.g., "God meant for *me* to take the last donut because I didn't have breakfast") or use spiritual explanations to justify behavior (e.g., "God told me to dump my marriage and quit my job to grow in His image and likeness").[14]

Feeling afraid about surrendering to the will of God? You can take fearfulness as a sign your faith tanks are running on near-empty. Refill them by recalling instances in your life when, having reached the end of your rope, you let go completely and everything turned out just fine. Remember, a leap of faith is not jumping from point A to point B; it's jumping from point A.

Is your calling coming from God or a supernatural prankster who has your number? Yes, you can tell the real from the unreal. An authentic call will give you a sense of clarity and certainty in the face of opposition from others and disturbance of your own. It's entirely possible to know you're being called and to feel less than thrilled about it.

ANGELS WE HAVE HEARD (MAYBE) ON HIGH

Every spiritual tradition recognizes the powerful pull of dark forces seeking to divert travelers from the path of righteous action. But don't expect to be detoured by a little red entity sporting horns and a pitchfork. You could be led astray by circumstances or someone who seems to be benign. You could also be horribly distracted by visions, voices, and light shows. The illumination may in fact be blinding.

Yes, it's true that saints throughout the ages have experienced all sorts of cosmically fabulous stuff—bleeding roses, crying statues, ecstatic giggles, keeling over in a buzzing burst of electrical energy. And it's entirely possible you, too, may be part of this great mystic tradition. Nevertheless, proceed with caution whenever you believe you've received direction in supernatural form.

What you thought was a sign from God may be heralding something steeped in darkness rather than divine light, and you've been led to a dead end or, if you're lucky, merely a cul-de-sac. Take a tip from experienced Seekers who know it's wise to check with spiritually mature souls about directions—supernatural and otherwise—appearing to be coming from God.

"Souls should not content themselves with these supernatural apprehensions, but strive to forget them for the sake of being free."

—St. John of the Cross—

CONTEMPLATIVE WRITING EXERCISE
"DO UNTO OTHERS..."

Here's an exercise, one grounded in your own experience of being supported during difficult times, to help you figure out how to answer the inner call to service.

First, list major life challenges and losses that have led you to grow emotionally and spiritually. Next, note all the ways you were supported during these periods. Include the big stuff, like the money your future ex-in-laws gave you without expectation of repayment, as well as big little stuff like the pint of fresh raspberries your neighbor left on your doorstep. Now, take a look at what's on these lists and write out whatever comes to mind as you answer these questions:

- Which acts of generosity or kindness meant the most to me?
- What made these gestures so meaningful?
- How can I give to others what was given to me?

"God is not interested in what happens to turn out to be good or in what appears to be good. He is interested in the purpose for which a thing is done."

—St. John Damascene—

Boost your inspiration quotient by reading about people who have made a difference. Case in point: while laid low with a battle wound in 1521, Ignatius Loyola relieved boredom by reading about saints. Look how *he* turned out! Stories about community activists and social reformers are inspiring. Heck, you don't even have to plow through an entire book (other than this one). You can flip through magazines or surf the Internet (e.g., Mashable.com/Watercooler, Bored Panda) to read about ordinary people doing extraordinary things.

Expand your search for service and significance beyond the corporeal world. Dreams, especially reoccurring ones, can provide a map to your future, so start keeping a dream journal. Before crawling into bed, pray that you're shown how to be useful. If you don't normally remember dreams, also ask to be given the gift of remembering what's revealed. The best time to record dreams is while you're neither totally asleep nor totally awake. Note: If the physical act of writing feels too disruptive, whisper your dreams into a voice activated recorder.

> "*I slept and dreamt that life was joy.*
> *I awoke and saw that life was service.*
> *I acted and behold, service was joy.*"
> —Tagore—

Your mind and soul are in cahoots with your body, so pay attention to your physical status.[15] Consider heart palpitations and stomach flutters, all of which are common signs of excitement, tangible ways to discern an authentic call. Conversely, feeling logy is a pretty decent sign something is not quite right. So is feeling stiff, achy, or sore for no apparent physiological reason. While you're at it, let the body-mind connection clue you into motives that are, shall we say, somewhat less than noble—like you're really excited about the possibility of being lauded for your infinite goodness.

Specific skills, like being able to drive a backhoe or remove tonsils, are obviously valuable, but many organizations neither need to require this level of skill from volunteers. More often than not, having someone answer the phones without attitude or make deliveries without stopping off for coffee along the way is considered a huge blessing. You can serve and serve well without having snazzy specialties.

OFFER GIFTS OR ENTER THE FIRE OF TRANSFORMATION?

Most people, when either pressed or moved to serve others, respond by offering expertise, experience, and talents. After all, why let these gifts go to waste? You, in fact, may be reluctant to volunteer for anything because you don't have anything spectacular to offer. Well, here's some good news: in *bona fide* spiritual communities, serving from one's worldly strengths is rarely encouraged, at least not for quite a while. If anything, highly trained and educated aspirants are usually given the most ego-deflating tasks in the joint.

Go ahead, ask any monk no longer observing silence what he or she did during the first few heady years of monastery or ashram life. What you'll hear are stories about the spiritual benefits of such mind-numbing work as scrubbing toilets, peeling tubers, raking leaves, or in these high-tech days, mailing list management.[16]

Sooner rather than later, Seekers stuck with scut work are forced to look at all sorts of freaky stuff like attachments, arrogance, pride, and willfulness—just to name a few things separating self from Self and the Divine.

If you're wondering what on earth those lofty learnings have to do with deciding whether to participate in your community, workplace, school, or religious organization, you might consider that plain and simple service will help you discover how much patience and humility you possess without entering a cloistered community to find out.

> *"The purpose of life is to increase the*
> *warm heart. Think of other people. Serve other*
> *people sincerely. No cheating."*
> —Dalai Lama—

Before choosing a place to focus your energy, talk to several longtime volunteers about the ecstasies and agonies of doing service work in general. Over a leisurely cup of something or a long rambling walk, ask:

- Why did you get involved with service?
- How did you choose where to get involved?
- What do you like most about volunteering?
- Are there any aspects of this work you can't stand?

Don't worry too much if you act on your own will before getting around to knowing or doing God's. Just make sure you're doing something for the greater good of all and you can't go to wrong.

> *"Do God's will as if it were your will, and God will*
> *accomplish your will as if it were His own."*
> —Rabbi Gamaliel—

Your motives for serving will have an impact on your total experience, so become as clear as you possibly can from the get-go. Make a date with yourself a few months down the line to check your motives again. Are they the same? Have they changed? If so, "how" and "why" are always good questions to contemplate.

CONTEMPLATIVE WRITING EXERCISE
"CREATE IN ME A CLEAN HEART..."

Others may have a hidden agenda, but not you! Your motives for serving are beatifically pure, or so you'd like to believe. Well, you might want to take a closer look at that particular belief system to make sure you're on the side of the angels. Use this exercise to sort through your intentions by writing immediate gut-level answers to these questions:

- Are there any debts to individuals or society I feel the need
  to repay?
- Who am I hoping will be the greatest beneficiary of my service?
- Why do I want to get involved in service at this age and stage of my life?

Don't be too surprised if, in the process of doing this, some terribly human motives and expectations are revealed— like wanting recognition, spiritual brownie points, or something suitably saintly to put on your résumé. You always have the option of choosing a form or environment for service that will clear and clean your heart.

CHAPTER 3

Discovering Your Place

INTRODUCTION

Now that the call to serve others is reverberating in your heart and mind, it's time to find a place to donate time, talents, and quite possibly, money. Maybe you'll be like those graced enough to know exactly what to do and where. While you are praying, meditating, writing in your journal, or dragging garbage to the curb on a starry night, you experience a few moments of transcendental clarity. The very next day you make a few phone calls and within a week have found the service environment of your dreams.

Maybe you, like many others, will stumble into service. Your employer announces comp time for anyone doing community service work. A friend needs surgery, and, for the first time, you understand the value of donating blood. One of the worst hurricanes in recent history wreaks havoc an hour away, and you decide to show up in hip boots to help. As you participate, you discover yourself feeling more and more open to life and Spirit. What was supposed to be a one-time stint becomes something much more.

Or you're like those stumped about what to do next. So intent are you on being in alignment with God's will that you have trouble moving forward into action. Should you find a place that will appreciate your skill set, or is that too egotistical? Should you serve where you already know other volunteers, or is that too comfy? Should you find a service gig requiring a weekly time commitment, or is that unrealistic, given your schedule? Should you do something locally, or is that too insular? Should you investigate something globally oriented, or is that too grandiose? Clearly, you could make yourself fairly nuts at this stage. Fortunately, you won't have to because tips in this chapter will help you decide where to serve.

CHAPTER TIPS

Cultivate ideas for getting involved by scanning local, regional, national, or international news in a more focused way. As you behold evidence of tragedy, waste, abuse, and simple ignorance in the world, get into the habit of asking yourself:

- What would make a difference?
- How might *I* make a difference?

> "If you can't feed 100 people, then just feed one."
> —Mother Teresa—

The Internet has made seeking and finding service opportunities easier than ever before. Once, you'd have to scan "blue pages" or "Yellow Pages" of the telephone book (remember those?). Now if you want to volunteer at your local food pantry, simply type, "food pantry, volunteer opportunities, [your location]" or, "donating blood [your location]" and so forth into a search engine.

Social media makes it easier to explore service opportunities— and then apply for them. On LinkedIn, for example, you may list the types of service activities and/or causes you're interested in directly on your profile. LinkedIn, a social network for professionals, will alert organizations seeking volunteers about your interests—and vice versa. On Facebook, you can publically share your status as an organ donor.

Some organizations are great places to give money, but you wouldn't want to serve there. Figure this out by generating a list of charities and service organizations whose missions you admire and want to support, and then investigate them more carefully. Check out their governance structure, ask around about how they treat volunteers, take a look at their finances. Do this due diligence, and then sort them according to whether you want to donate services, goods, or money.

Contact a charity already getting your bucks to ask about other ways to become involved. Gather information about what's needed; then sort through the options at your leisure. Be careful about service work of any kind that results in a major commitment on the basis of one well-meaning and possibly impulsive phone call.

What helps you restore soul and spirit? Combine service work for others along with R & R[17] for yourself by looking into gigs at museums, theaters, concert halls, nature preserves, or community playgrounds. Maybe a local yoga teacher needs an assistant to help schlep mats, cushions, and blankets to the class he teaches at a nearby prison.

Double your pleasure and satisfaction by putting hobbies to good use. Help plant, weed, and water a community garden; read to children in a pediatric unit at the local hospital; pilot a plane for an environmental watchdog organization; groom dogs at the local shelter; groom horses at a therapeutic riding center; record books on tape for the visually impaired and dyslexic; teach halfway house residents how to shop for bargains.

Get practice in your chosen career by serving while still a student, especially if you're studying law or medicine. Your skills will be welcomed by community-based clinics, and you may also be able to earn course credit for your efforts.

If you've left the practice of law, medicine, or architecture because you couldn't stand professional constraints, put your skills to excellent use for those who will appreciate them

without anyone expecting you to be "billable." There are
organizations specializing in matching doctors and lawyers
with other organizations who need—often desperately—
volunteers with your expertise.

Age is no barrier to serving others. If you're semi- or totally
retired, you probably have more time available anyway. That,
plus skills acquired from years in the workforce, makes you
most valuable. Some organizations specialize in matching
retirees with those who could use mentoring in specific areas
of business.

Enjoy animals more than people? No problem. Animal lovers
can serve by doing everything from scooping cat poop at the
local shelter to raising Seeing Eye dogs—and beyond. There
are plenty of ways to alleviate animal suffering without liberating rats from the local neurophysiology lab.

Don't underestimate the power of serving in ways that create
beauty and laughter. Nursing homes, hospitals, shelters,
rehabilitation centers, and schools benefit enormously from
contributions involving, and in turn fostering, creative expression. Your talents as an artist, musician, dancer, writer, needle
crafter, storyteller, or comic are as valuable as any of the more
prosaic ways of serving.

CONTEMPLATIVE WRITING EXERCISE
KNOW THYSELF IN THE WORLD

Over the years you've probably filled out dozens, if not hundreds, of forms requesting vital statistics. Indeed, it's practically impossible to accomplish anything these days without locating yourself more or less precisely in the social world. Well, here you're invited to do so again, only this time *you* will be the one scrutinizing data.

In addition to filling in facts, write responses to thought ticklers in each category. After completing this exercise, not only will you have a handy list of who you are but also a sense of whatever meaning you load onto each sociological variable. Now what? Use this information to help evaluate service options.

- **Sex and Gender**
  How does being female or male shape the way you look at situations and people? How comfortable (or combative) are you with members of the opposite sex? How comfortable (or combative) are you in the presence of non-binary gender?
- **Age**
  How easily are you able to interact with people of all ages?
- **Race/ethnicity**
  How does your racial-ethnic identity shape the way you look at situations and people? How comfortable (or combative) are you in interracial or multiethnic situations? How important is it for you to be with people of your own race or ethnicity?
- **Marital Status**
  How does your marital status shape the way you look at situations and people?
- **Education**
  How important is education to you? How do you feel (or behave) around people who have more (or less) education than you?

- **Occupation**
  How does what you do to earn a living shape the way you live?
- **Income**
  How does the amount you earn shape your lifestyle? How do you feel (or behave) around people who make more (or less) money than you?
- **Health Status**
  How have health challenges faced by you or loved ones shaped your attitudes and beliefs?
- **Religion**
  How has your religious upbringing (or lack thereof) shaped the way you look at situations and people? How important is it for you to be with people who share your beliefs?

> "*Never doubt that a small group of thoughtful, devoted citizens can change the world; indeed, it is the only thing that ever has.*"
> —Margaret Mead—

Can't stand where you work, or the industry as a whole, but can't afford to quit? Nothing wrong with channeling your ire into a little guerrilla service or philanthropy in the direction of causes to offset whatever you think are skewed and screwy corporate values.

How much time should you spend doing service work? It's more a question of how much time *can* you devote to service work while sustaining life on this planet. Calculate this by subtracting from the number of hours per week (168) the amount of time you need to spend on:

- basic living (e.g., sleeping, eating, personal hygiene, shopping, cooking, cleaning);

- paid employment and/or formal education;

- family or social obligations (e.g., intimate relationships, childcare, friendships); and

- personal growth (e.g., hobbies, devotions, psychotherapy, life coaching).

The amount of time remaining is the time you realistically have available. Keep in mind that most volunteer activities require a minimum amount of regular service. Be sure to account for the time it takes to travel to and from your do-good gig. As with any other budget, if the amount you come up with is too small, you'll need to change time allocations in other categories.

Use service work to enhance your marriage and family quality time by seeking opportunities that engage your spouse and perhaps your kids. Just having a discussion about serving others as a couple or an entire family can expand everyone's capacity for generosity, empathy, and togetherness. Family-oriented service also provides a valuable way to practice the art of negotiation and compromise. If picking up roadside trash doesn't appeal to everyone, maybe participating in a program bringing toys to homeless, sick, or physically challenged children will.

STARTING SERVICE
THE ULTIMATE PRAYER

My Lord God,
I have no idea where I am going.
I do not see the road ahead of me.
I cannot know for certain where it will end.
Nor do I really know myself,
and the fact that I think
I am following your will
does not mean that I am actually doing so.
But I believe
that the desire to please you
does in fact please you.
And I hope I have that desire in all that I am
doing.
I hope that I will never do anything apart
from that desire.
And I know that if I do this
you will lead me by the right road,
though I may know nothing about it.
Therefore I will trust you always
though I may seem to be lost
and in the shadow of death.
I will not fear,
for you are ever with me,
and You will never leave me
to face my perils alone.

—Thomas Merton

EXTREME RECYCLING: DONATING BLOOD AND GUTS

You dutifully park bundled papers and magazines at the curb weekly, along with empty cans and bottles that you, for one, have the decency to rinse out. Thanks to the Salvation Army, your outgrown clothes and unwanted housewares find the gift of extended life in someone else's home. During the winter, you stash eggshells, carrots scrapings, potato peels, and other cooking detritus in your freezer until it's warm enough to compost. Clearly, you comprehend the value of recycling. Now, how about kicking it up a notch to donate blood while you're still among the living—and vital organs and tissues after you're not?

Human blood, which is one of the few physiological artifacts that can't be replicated in a lab, is always in short supply. Blood donation will take less than an hour out of your life to extend someone else's by many.

As for organs and tissues, there's always a major demand for kidneys, hearts, lungs, livers, corneas, sclera (white part of the eye) pancreases, middle ears, pituitary glands, skin, and bone marrow. (Bone marrow is harvested from living donors.) While you can get temporary artificial heart parts, ultimately you'll need the real-life thing from a dead person.

If your reluctance to donate is based on religious principles, concerns about how you'll look at your own funeral, anonymity, or—in the case of blood donations—pain, you can relax.

The major world religions view organ donation—the gift of life—as the ultimate charitable contribution one human can make to another. Perhaps the conversation you really need to have is one about the body-soul connection and what you truly believe about what happens (and where "you" go) after death. Have this chat with a spiritual advisor.

If tradition calls for an open casket and you want to worry about something, focus on your outfit. Organs and tissues are removed by sterile procedure that keeps the rest of your body intact. You won't be disfigured, and—ignore science thrillers—you'll be thoroughly, completely, and irrevocably departed before anything is surgically removed.

No need to worry about anyone claiming to have your feelings and interests if your heart ends up in his or her chest. Transplant teams keep identities of donors and recipients unknown to everyone involved (unless otherwise stipulated), and only general information is released. What you should not keep secret is your wish to be an organ donor. *Signing a donor card or checking the boxes on your driver's license isn't enough.* Your next of kin still has to provide written consent, so make sure your desire to be an organ donor is clearly known. Even so, there are no guarantees. Your wishes can be overruled by the living, but depending on the ultimate spiritual reality, you may or may not know this has happened.

From one donor, six lifesaving organs and nine vital tissues can be recovered or transplanted. This blood and guts has to come from someone; why not you?

Your marriage isn't perfect? You can learn that you're not alone while helping others! Most faith communities sponsor marriage enrichment programs staffed by volunteers willing to honestly share their experiences with couples who are either planning marriage or newly married. Couples who have the grace and guts to serve this way usually find their own marriage enhanced in the process.

Single, but don't wanna be? Choose service environments where you'll meet like-minded singles. Count on learning oodles about someone's personality and style by working side-by-side on a committee or project. What someone brings to a potluck supper can reveal more than a dozen dates.

If you're a parent and do nothing more than commit to teaching your kids how to act with integrity and honesty; to feel and express empathy, generosity, and kindness; to consider the needs of others; and to become good citizens, then you can proudly claim you've found an invaluable place to serve—your family.

CONTEMPLATIVE WRITING EXERCISE
AS YOU WOULD HAVE DONE UNTO YOURSELF...

Clueless about where to get involved? Perhaps your notion of service work has been tainted by a childhood filled with forced Scout marches through nursing homes. Or hearing the words "community involvement" conjures up images of incidents you'd rather forget. Complete this exercise to help you find a place to serve.

First, list social issues that interest you the most. Don't strive for coherence—"displaced homemakers" can appear on the same list as "hospice" and "wildlife preservation." On a separate sheet, so as not to be distracted by your first list, catalog pet peeves without worrying about the profundity factor. Feel free to note your ongoing gripe about unsynchronized traffic lights and ugly landscaping in front of the local senior center, as well as weightier matters such as the convoluted nature of voter registration.

Your next task involves the careful, contemplative look at your list with an eye—and heart— for commonalities. Is there anything on the pet peeve list that might be a subset of your favorite social issues? Do you spy patterns indicating a preference for dealing with individuals rather than groups? Use whatever you discover to narrow the universe of possibilities.

Any time you want to immediately up-level your spiritual attainment, find a service commitment at either end point of life. There's nothing quite like being present at birth or death to goose your own spiritual growth. Both processes offer enough mystery, grace, and gore to keep you hiking the spiritual path.

Know your preference and tolerance for different types of organizations. Maybe you're unfazed by the hoopla within bulky bureaucracies. Perhaps you're creeped out by the intimacy of small groups. Or you prefer participatory democracy to a benevolent dictatorship. How the organization is structured will set much of the tone and help determine your future happiness, so find this out in advance.

Even if the organization has been around forever, make an effort to research it thoroughly before volunteering. This goes double if you're planning to donate money. Take time to:

- Read whatever pamphlets or reports the organization has issued about itself, including its annual financial report.
- Talk with others about what they've heard—or actually know—about the organization.
- Get a tour that includes people as well as facilities.

Pay attention to more subtle indicators during site visits. The most upscale facility can be a snake pit and the worst dump close to heaven on earth, so zoom in on vibes. Notice if the scene feels warm, authentic, slightly odd, or downright creepy. Enlist or flee accordingly.

Before leaving any site visit, request contact information for volunteers willing to talk about their experiences. Make sure you follow up with a friendly conversation during which you get the real scoop. Perhaps the organization is great, but the executive director is not. Or the organization is a bureaucratic nightmare, but the people and cause are fabulous enough to make it worthwhile. Maybe Wednesday is the absolute worst day to volunteer. Better to find out *before* signing up.

Be persistent about contacting the service organization until you get a response. Take as a given the fact that most nonprofit organizations are understaffed and underfunded, which is why it may take ages upon ages for you to hear back from anyone, but also maybe why you should not volunteer. Maybe.

It has been weeks, and still no one is calling you back? Not even an email response? Your options:

- View the lack of response as an opportunity to practice patience, compassion, and a renewed commitment to be of service. Keep trying.

- View the lack of response as an indicator of organizational dysfunction that will eventually sour you on the entire cause. Pick another arena for service.

What can you do to make a difference where you already work? Maybe it's time to persuade your boss, the restaurateur, to donate leftover food to a homeless shelter. Perhaps other car mechanics at the shop will volunteer to service cars for single (and highly stressed-out) mothers at your house of worship. How about assembling your creative team to develop fundraising materials for struggling nonprofit organizations?

If you're the owner and boss, more power to you! It doesn't matter how big or small a company, join other smart CEOs who realize the human value of corporate giving in various forms. You can do anything from sponsoring a blood drive to donating a percentage of company profits to a national organization. Zoom in on something you feel ardent about. Find out what sort of service engages your employees by conducting a survey of their interests. In addition:

- Offer first dibs on used but serviceable office furniture and equipment to schools, literacy programs, or other charitable organizations with those needs.[18]

- Actively recruit and hire people with physical, mental, and learning disabilities; alcoholics and drug addicts actively working a program of recovery; and ex-convicts who deserve another chance.

- Open your conference rooms, computer facilities, and employee gym to community programs needing space to meet, train staff, or deliver services.

HOW I SPENT MY SUMMER VACATION

You used to lay out in the sun reading trashy novels and spending too much on meals. When that got old, you discovered the world of personal growth retreats and spent many happy hours hanging out with your Inner Child. Perhaps it's time to take the journey within out into the world. You can easily find service vacation opportunities lasting anywhere from weeks to months and costing anything between a couple of hundred and a few thousand tax-deductible dollars.

The fact you're no longer living your regular life with its regular work and regular Netflix binge-watching is what makes this a "vacation." In reality, you'll be working your *tuchas* off in what may be less-than-pleasant conditions, which is why you'll need to examine expectations in advance.

Take, for example, the prospect of being immersed in indigenous culture. What seems grand from the cozy comfort of your breakfast nook may feel entirely different upon arrival. You may find yourself bedding down in a sleeping bag, squeezing into your host family's already crowded bedroom, or lodged in a local hotel with hot and cold running palmetto bugs. Local culture may gift you with intestinal viruses.

Without a doubt, you'll have memorable moments to post on social media; they just won't be like anything you imagined. But isn't that the point? The same old, same old self-indulgence just isn't cutting it anymore. It's time to do something different, and there are any number of organizations that would be delighted to put you to work around the world.

"There is nothing small in the service of God."

—St. Francis DeSales—

THE GIG IS RIGHT FOR YOU IF...

- You're so inspired by and dedicated to The Cause that you don't care what it takes to get involved.
- You have all the time in the world to serve, even if much of that time includes sitting in meetings where your contributions are ignored. Simply being there works for you.
- You not only respect but like the people in charge—their values, dedication, and human decency. You are, after all, never too old for wonderful role models.
- You experience satisfaction despite whatever frustrations and disappointments quickly—or gradually—emerge. As far as you're concerned, growing emotionally and spiritually is what it's all about.

THIS GIG IS SO WRONG FOR YOU IF...

- You feel entirely too overwhelmed by the enormity of what needs to be done. Whatever issue or situation the organization or agency is tackling seems too much for you to handle.
- You're constantly awash with waves of emotion too gigantic to safely surf. When you're not feeling rage at the massive Unfairness of It All, you're sobbing with grief.
- You not only start dreading the prospect of showing up, but you unconsciously—or consciously—act out by arriving late or calling in sick or too busy.
- You discover there's truly absolutely nothing for you to do.

Notice whenever your best efforts seem to go nowhere. You may be moving against the will of God and order of the Universe if everything relative to the service you want to get into is difficult and aggravating. Your appointment with the program director keeps getting canceled; your start date and time are switched a half-dozen times; things come together only to fall completely apart. This is not going with the flow—but swimming upstream.

SO YOU'VE BEEN ASKED TO JOIN THE BOARD

If you have a track record for doing good, having big bucks, or being able to influence others, then at some point you'll probably be invited to serve on the Board of Directors (BOD). Proceed with caution; do not say "yes" immediately. First, you want to do some serious organizational spelunking as well as soul-searching.

An invitation to serve on the BOD of a nonprofit organization is always a mixed blessing. Unless you're so incredibly well-known that the mere presence of your name on a letterhead will elicit gasps of awe and approval for The Cause, watch out.

Dinky organizations, struggling to survive, will probably suck the life force out of you within six months. Plan on attending lots of meetings, including ones characterized as "emergencies" that probably aren't. The Executive Director will view you as a personal savior or antichrist. Count on feeling like both when it inevitably comes time to fire everybody allegedly in charge. You'll meet in someone's rumpus room or cram into the organization's conference room/storage closet—late at night. Forget designer coffee and treats unless toting your own. The annual BOD retreat will be held on a Saturday morning at the local elementary school.

Large, established organizations will expect you to contribute money and raise more to boot, which means you'll be hitting up your friends and colleagues on a regular basis. This won't be a problem if you consort with wealthy generous folks who, by the way, will be hitting *you* up for contributions to *their* favorite causes. As for meetings, you'll probably have to show up at least three or four times a year for an entire day and, more likely, a long weekend. And there's also monthly committee work! Yes, the real work of directing big, established organizations is done in committees where you may have some clout—on your time and dime, of course. Good news: the annual BOD retreat will be at a resort. Bad news: you may not have time to play golf, take a yoga class, or get a facial.

Depending on the governance structure of the organization, you may end up with something called "fiduciary responsibility." These official scary-sounding words are indeed official and scary. Basically, they mean that in the event of some financial screw up by staff, board members are responsible. This is why you'll need to study the annual report, examine financial records, and make sure they have liability insurance before you agree to serve.

So much for generalities! Get specifics by asking smart questions in advance. You may decide being an active volunteer, contributor, or both makes a lot more sense.

"Ambition kills spirituality."

—Paramanada—

Before saying "yes" to being a board member, talk with existing and former board members about serving on the BOD. Don't be afraid to ask:

- How big is the board and how is it structured?
- How are committee assignments made?
- How efficiently and effectively is the board managed?

- Does the organization have sufficient liability insurance?
- How is policy made and implemented?
- How much will I be expected to contribute and raise?
- How often and where do you meet?
- What you like best and least about this board?
- Why should I become a board member?

THREE GOOD REASONS TO GIVE MONEY INSTEAD

- In the presence of social problems, you tend to act out by becoming snappish or mopey instead of pitching in.
- As it is, you're already neglecting your family, friends, and Fido.
- You have more money than time.

Know your financial limitations. Make a realistic appraisal of your circumstances before deciding how much money you'll contribute to one or more causes. Generally speaking, you could probably stand to fork over more money than you think you can afford, but giving to the point where you become financially destabilized is foolishness, arrogance, or both.

Two approaches to donating money:

1. Tie financial contributions to your service activities. In other words, give money to causes and organizations that are also beneficiaries of your time. This

will give you a stronger sense of commitment and, if it's an important factor, influence.

2. Give your time to causes and organizations that are near and dear to your heart. Give money to those in which you believe but cannot show up to serve in person.

Check first with an accountant or financial planner about the tax ramifications before making substantial donations. In some circumstances, it will make more fiscal sense to donate stock instead of cash. If really big bucks are involved, you might want to consider setting up your own foundation. Consider the spiritual growth available to you by *not* naming it after yourself or your family unless the name recognition will enhance the cause.

> *"The wealthy…consider their greatest gain what they spend to alleviate the distress of others."*
> —St. Leo the Great—

Keep scrupulous written records of anything you spend during the course of donating service. This includes mileage and transportation costs; meals and lodging; unreimbursed expenses; and the costs and upkeep of uniforms. Just about everything is tax-deductible. Check with an accountant for prevailing rates.

TITHING

Tithing is a practice of setting aside a portion of income for the express purpose of helping others. The tithe was first developed to support the Levitical priesthood, then others in the community. Today, tithing ten percent of net income is generally viewed as an obligation of all who belong to the Christian faith community, paid to and dispersed by the church. Tithing, although in a somewhat different form, is central to Islam as well.

Almsgiving (*zakat*) is the third of the five pillars of Islam and so closely aligned with prayer (*salat*) that devout Muslims view the failure to tithe as a sign of unbelief in God. While Muslims acknowledge the value of voluntary almsgiving (*sadaqah*) to help the needy, *zakat* is not optional. If this lifetime is a test, ignoring *zakat* is a good way to flunk. Islam's holy scripture, the Qur'an, reveals dire circumstances at the final Judgment Day for those who hoard gold, silver, crops, and livestock.

Unlike Christian forms of charity or Judaism's *tzedakah*, *zakat* is an obligatory welfare tax in the form of an annual tithe of 2.5% of all accumulated *wealth and assets.* The Qur'an specifies the redistribution of *zakat* to ameliorate economic inequities among Muslims; free debtors, slaves, and prisoners of war; attract converts and support new ones; help stranded Muslim wayfarers; pay wages to those involved in collecting *zakat*; and support and defend the spread of Islam. The precise calculation of *zakat* has been sorely challenged by the emergence of paper money and other stuff.

Despite some obvious key differences with regard to tithing, Christians and Muslims share the belief that everything is ultimately owned by God and we are merely stewards. The quality of stewardship is a matter of heart, law, or both.

Small change can really add up to something. Every three months, on a day when you either have nothing better to do or want to procrastinate, collect pennies, nickels, dimes, and quarters from your dresser drawer, car ashtray, or huge jar you once thought would make a great terrarium. Then, after spinning it through your supermarket's electronic coin counter, transform it into a charitable contribution.

Instead of blowing money on extravagant gifts no one wants or needs, consider making charitable contributions in the recipient's name. Major charitable organizations will send a tasteful notification card via snail mail—or you can do all of this online. Do not, however, attempt this with your own kids. They'll only get sulky and need expensive therapy later to complain about familial neglect. Adults are more likely to feel touched by the effort and possibly relieved.

Collect clothes you hoped would fit again, duplicate kitchen appliances acquired at marriage; power tools that ended up in your garage after the divorce; all sports equipment your kids were dying to have and then ditched within months; ugly furniture you inherited. There's almost nothing service organizations like the Salvation Army, Goodwill Industries, or the Vietnam Veterans of America won't take off your hands. Many organizations will arrive at your home with vans and big, burly guys to cart off perfectly good junk. Don't forget to get a tax deduction receipt!

Still reading print magazines? Instead of tossing them into recycling bins, bring relief to those stuck in hospital waiting areas with ratty, out-of-date magazines by donating current castoffs. Some hospitals provide drop-off bins outside the main entrance. Make sure donations are in relatively good condition, meaning you can rip out a few recipes or coupons, but not the end of the story. Remember to remove your address label to protect your privacy.

Does the stash of old high-tech equipment make your basement look like an electronics superstore? Depending on the age of the equipment, fledgling organizations will welcome computers in good shape. Police departments in many major cities will accept cell phone donations, reprogramming them to call 911 exclusively and giving them to those who may be in emergency situations (e.g., senior citizens, domestic violence victims). With a little bit of online research, you may be able to find organizations refurbishing old computer equipment as their ministry.

Teach your kids good stewardship—the proper management of Divine abundance—by asking them to set aside a portion of their allowance for a charity they choose. As an incentive, create a matching fund where you kick in an additional amount for every dollar they set aside.

CHARITY BEGINS AT HOME

It may feel so much more virtuous to help others, but giving everything from emotional support to practical assistance must begin at home. Heaven points are deducted—if not totally canceled out—for assisting others to the neglect of one's own family and kin. Sacred texts are chock full of admonitions about such not-so-benign neglect. Alas, this very human problem persists to this day.

Sometimes these disconnects show up as participating in literacy programs but ducking out of the kids homework; cooking up a storm to stock the church freezer and subjecting the family to take-out; working for the environment while using enough paper products to deforest the Pacific Northwest; or pounding nails for Habitat for Humanity but ignoring that elephant-sized (and shaped) stain on the living room ceiling. Every day, throughout the world, therapists listen to progeny of Lord and Lady Bountiful types complain about inattentive do-gooder parents.

So before rushing off to be of service, take time for an unflinching look at that microcosm of the world's pressing social issues—your family. Knowing and nurturing your place at home can only serve to enhance your sense of authentic place in the world at large. Any resistance you may feel to focusing first on those near and dear is to be taken as a sign it's once again time to scrutinize your motives for serving out the world.

CHAPTER 4

Becoming and Being Involved

INTRODUCTION

Long before you arrived on the scene, assuming you're not a founding member, the service environment in which you've plunked yourself had already created a culture. Values and beliefs had evolved to create a context for action. Embedded within this culture is a social structure, with rules established to regulate action within this context.

If any of this sounds vaguely familiar, it's because you've just read the short form of an opening lecture for Sociology 101.[19] Now, as back then when your mind wandered during that undergraduate class, you're probably wondering what all this has to do with you. Well, just like your exasperated professor told you back then, I hasten to remind you that culture and society are worth studying. Learning everything you can about them will help you navigate more comfortably and rebel more strategically in any given social situation. This is true whether you find yourself in a cozy commune or bloated bureaucracy, a strictly regimented small group or a wildly disorganized social services agency.

Try not to worry about those you're called to serve. Hopefully, you'll receive training to help you interact successfully with them. Even if you don't, you've entered the situation with an open mind and heart, right? You've gone through a discernment process (see, Chapter 2: Discerning the Call), you found a place to serve (see, Chapter 3: Discovering Your Place), and you're so willing to become involved that you'll welcome communication glitches and organizational snafus as opportunities to grow in patience, humility, and faith (see, Chapter 1: Service as a Spiritual Practice).

But what about everyone and everything else—supervisors, other volunteers, staff meetings, and the parking situation? Get ready to embrace countless opportunities to grow in obedience, perseverance, and trust. Do not be at all surprised if your open mind and heart slam shut as you encounter situations and personalities that remind you of other people and places, like where you work for pay. And just like employment environments, what's unwritten and unsaid is as important, if not more so, than what's documented in official materials. You'll need to know this stuff, or at least how to find someone to guide you. Tips in this chapter will provide some orientation to working happily and successfully shoulder-to-shoulder—instead of grimly hands-to-throat—in just about any service environment.[20]

CHAPTER TIPS

You zeroed in on an area for service and researched where to enlist. Now, saturate yourself with information about "the cause" itself. Get educated about key historical, social, political, and economic issues, as well as central players. Were key participants well-heeled do-gooders or street brawlers? Did funding once come from organized religious charities? Who now "owns" the issues? Are those being served receiving attention from special interest groups? Not only will learning history help you get a sense of what's truly needed but it will help you manage situations that, without deep background, may not make a lot of sense.[21]

Ensure your own safety. Unless you're an adrenaline junkie (which certainly deserves closer scrutiny), make sure you feel physically safe wherever you serve and certainly traveling to and from the site. Feeling terror or even low-level fear about the setting itself will diminish your ability to be useful.

Agree to serve on a trial basis. Establish a mutually acceptable period of time to check out the setting, staff, and other volunteers. Committing to at least one month and preferably three will give you—and them—an opportunity to explore the match. Doing this before making a long-term commitment will significantly reduce the possibility of hard feelings if things don't work out.

Clarify your own availability to reduce possible confusion. Before starting your service, let those in charge know about time constraints due to family and work responsibilities. Don't forget to mention that month-long annual vacation, your tradition of observing major holy days, and the chronic illness that flattens you whenever it rains.

> *"Do all the good you can. By all the means you can. In all the ways you can. In all the places you can. At all the times you can. To all the people you can. As long as ever you can."*
> —John Wesley—

When scheduling, remember to allow for your biorhythms and overall energy levels. Go ahead and volunteer for the midnight shift if nighttime is the right time for you. Do not volunteer for high-stress assignments at the end of your grueling work week.

Start a prayer journal when you begin a new type or place of service. Note what you're being called upon to do, and record any thoughts, feelings, and attitudes that emerge. Hint: Use what you've recorded as a foundation for prayers of petition in which you call upon the Divine for personal support and guidance, as well as for intercessory prayers, in which you invoke help for others.

Unemployed? After the jolt of joblessness wears off, consider volunteering. It will give you something uplifting to do between interviews. You may end up serving somewhere

that will reveal your true calling or perhaps lead to full-time
employment.

Clarify in advance what you'll be doing. Find out as much as
you can about your role and the responsibilities along with it.
It doesn't matter whether you're on paid staff or a volunteer,
you'll want to know how—and if—these roles differ. Although it's no guarantee of certainty, try to get a written job
description. Write your own, if necessary.

Take an active role in making sure your time is used wisely.
Instead of waiting for the Powers That Be to get it together,
notice what needs to be done; then pitch in. Surely you can
figure out when the coffeepot needs cleaning, clothing needs
to be put on hangers, or an incessantly ringing phone needs
answering. Sometimes the question, "May I help?" is more
useful than asking, "How can I help?"

Ask for feedback, but be able to carry on without receiving any.
It's perfectly human to want acknowledgment and approval, but
needing warm fuzzies could be a problem, especially if the
organization is understaffed and overly pressured. Resolve to do
your best under any and all conditions—even if no one notices.

Are you receiving "feedback" or engaging in "processing"?
Feedback requires your willingness to receive another person's observations. You listen to what's being said as openly

and carefully as is humanly possible. No arguing! Processing requires at least two willing participants, both of whom exchange emotional information with honesty, courtesy, and respect. Each party has a chance to safely articulate what seems to be going on. No interrupting! Clarifying this distinction at the outset will help you understand your role and responsibility for the interaction.

> *"One of the principal acts of charity is to bear with our neighbor, and we must realize this undoubted truth, that the difficulties we have with our neighbors spring more from our own poorly mortified tempers than from anything else."*
> —St. Vincent de Paul—

After figuring out official and unofficial rules, contemplate your willingness to follow them. While volunteering is a more flexible way to participate, it's not without organizational constraints. In some settings, like prisons and hospitals, your physical well-being may depend on your level of obedience. If you love rebellion, let the cause you serve, rather than your behavior, provide the antiestablishment thrills.

SELFLESS SERVICE
THE ULTIMATE PRAYER

Lord, make me an instrument of your peace.
Where there is hatred, let me sow love,
Where there is injury, pardon,
Where there is doubt, faith,
Where there is despair, hope,
Where there is darkness, light,
Where there is sadness, joy.
O Divine Master, Grant that I may not so
much seek
To be consoled, as to console,
To be understood, as to understand,
To be loved, as to love,
For it is in giving that we receive;
It in pardoning parting that we are pardoned;
It is in dying that we are born to eternal life.

—*St. Francis of Assisi*

PLAYING BY THE RULES

Every organization has rules governing every facet of
on-site behavior in formal organizations. These rules are
usually available in writing either in a hefty notebook or
online as downloadable PDFs. You'll find everything you
need to know about when to show up, what to wear, where
to park, and how to wind your way through the organization's innards.

What won't be revealed are the real rules—the stuff of organizational culture that everyone "knows" or had darn well
better find out to survive. Rules behind the rules regulate
things like seating at meetings, access to higher ups, speaking
out, and whether it's okay to use any old, unoccupied desk.

Learning informal structure is key to survival in complex organizations; this is true in simpler settings as well. Many organizational cognoscenti would, in fact, argue that survival in less formal environments is even more vitally connected to knowing the informal rules for action and interaction. No matter where you're located on or off the organizational chart, you're guaranteed to do better once you've learned how to see what doesn't readily show up and to hear what's left unspoken.

> *"The test of the real service to God is that it leaves*
> *behind it the feeling of humility."*
> —Baal Shem Tov—

What to wear? You might have to wear a uniform that looks ridiculous but solves the clothing issue. While you could rely on pure observation, asking is smarter because you could be misreading cultural clues. In some settings, staff dress is indistinguishable from that of clients. In others, clothing may help establish and maintain boundaries. There may be safety issues involved (e.g., everyone has to wear steel-toed shoes and bulletproof vests). In any event, neatness counts and so does good grooming. Clean up before showing up. Unless you really don't have to.

Don't hesitate to ask for guidance. Established service organizations are more likely to provide orientation and training you cannot count on receiving from younger, less organized groups. It's much safer to ask—or to do absolutely nothing—when you don't know what to do.

So you screwed up. Don't worry, you will not burn in eternal hell for being human if you:

- Promptly own up to what you did or didn't do.
- Clean up your mess or your part in creating a bigger one.
- Don't make the same mistake twice.

SPECIAL SITUATIONS: CAREGIVING

Big blessings to you if you feel called to provide care for those with serious and possibly terminal illnesses. More blessings if you're willing and able to do this for someone in your family. Because of your intimate involvement, you'll face different and possibly more extraordinary challenges than someone providing home healthcare professionally.

First, you simply must learn when and how to ask for additional assistance. For you, the growth may lie in asking for help. In addition to having relationships become deeper, richer, and more authentic:

- Your character is stretched and strengthened every time you muster the strength and maturity to ask for help.
- Your sense of comfort, safety, trust, and love will be enhanced by being helped by those you know.

Next, you'll need to learn how to make the best use of whatever help comes your way. Some (many?) family members may not, because of temperament, age, or life skills, pitch in to the extent you—or they—may want. Make the most of offers to help by taking these steps:

- Create a list of your concerns—real and imagined—then group them into categories. Your categories will include: household chores, errands, healthcare activities, personal care, and even "down" time.
- Generate a list of all tasks that will relieve those worries—even slightly! This will be a list of everything you need, from housecleaning to solitude, for a few hours or days.
- Create a list of everyone offering help and those you plan to ask, making note of their abilities and skills, in addition to their temperaments.
- Match caregivers to tasks based on what you need and who they are. Do not hesitate to offload tasks you don't like or find exhausting. Someone with more emotional distance might be better able to handle some personal hygiene tasks. Someone without major family responsibilities might be better suited to make a grocery store run. Keep for yourself tasks you enjoy or find relaxing.
- Write out the daily care schedule and necessary details so other caregivers don't need to pester you—although they might. The point is to relieve your stress, not add to it.

CONTEMPLATIVE WRITING EXERCISE
FORGIVENESS

When you started serving, you had every intention of being open, compassionate, generous, and loving. Alas, you've discovered that wherever you go, there you are—along with all your less-than-divine attributes. You're appalled to catch yourself being impatient, irritated, snarky, and petty. Not all the time, but enough to make you feel ashamed.[22] Hey, at least you've *noticed*! Cut yourself a break, and show yourself the generosity you to extend to others by exploring these questions:

> - What scared me?
> - Did I do my best under the circumstances?
> - What advice would I give a friend who is indulging in a similar self-flagellation spree?

Notice if and how you act out your discomfort. While negative body language could possibly be traced back to excess caffeine, something else is probably irking you. Use these behavioral warning signals to reexamine the setting and your involvement there:

- fidgeting

- wanting to flee

- muttering

- making snappy verbal comebacks

Count on having opinions and judgments as you listen to others, but remember: it's what you do with those opinions and judgments that counts. Psychospiritual growth lies in your ability to observe, neither expressing nor suppressing less-than-loving social commentary that may rattle through your skull mush or show up as body language.

*"Compassion is the only source of energy
that is useful and safe."*
—Thich Nhat Hanh—

Unless you always win card games because of your "poker face," learn to control how opinions and reactions are revealed in facial expressions.[23] No need to become a zombie, just more conscious of whatever negative nonverbal messages you might be transmitting. Since you can't catch yourself pulling a face in the mirror, ask a trusted colleague or friend to gently let you know when you're expressing a little too much emotion in the form of:

- frowning
- eye rolling
- smirking
- lip curling
- nostril flaring

Welcome silence, using it to gather information. There's actually a lot going on in any given group when no one is speaking. Zoom in on the general vibe. Has everything suddenly gotten heavy, agitated, or blank? What happens next? After that? Who in the group generally breaks the mood and how? What role do *you* play? What role, if any, do you *want* to play? By the way, choosing to opt out of group dynamics is still a form of involvement.

Be willing to not know. Let go of preconceived concepts, judgments, and answers to make space for new perceptions, ideas, and solutions. Consider the relief available from not knowing everything and having all the answers. How to let go? Adopt the spiritual practice of silently repeating or audibly murmuring the simple prayer, "Not my will, God, but yours" until it becomes part of your psyche and soul.

> "When all the knots that strangled the heart are loosened, the mortal becomes immortal."
> —The Upanishads—

ADVANCED COMMUNICATION

Communication comes in many forms, and, according to learning theorists, so do the ways people perceive and process information. Knowing your dominant learning style will help you do just about anything with significantly less effort and stress.[24]

- People always on the move and who enjoy physical activities like sports, exercise, dance, or ripping out bathroom tile are primarily *kinesthetic.*
- People who prefer spoken language (e.g., oral directions, podcasts) or who have a natural ear for music are primarily *auditory.*
- People who think in pictures, can put their ideas into charts and graphs, or are sensitive to nuances of color, texture, and shape are primarily *visual.*

No one is purely kinesthetic, auditory, or visual, but a blend of each mode of learning with one being dominant. Practically speaking, you'll communicate more effectively if you accommodate the learning style of the receiver. You may indeed have to provide a picture, write out lists, color code the calendar, or literally walk someone through an environment to get your point across. At the very least, use language that accommodates the listener's learning style.

- People who are primarily *kinesthetic* will respond to phrases such as "Imagine how the other person feels" or "I get the feeling that..."
- People who are primarily *auditory* will respond to phrases such as "Listen to this..." Or "Sounds to me as if..."
- People who are primarily *visual* will respond to phrases such as "I see your point..." Or "What if we look at it this way?"

Use seating to your and everyone else's advantage. Community builds more easily when people face one another. If seating is arranged classroom style, with all chairs facing forward, make a positive contribution to group dynamics by suggesting the room be reconfigured in a circle or U-shape. Any objections based on the size of the group can be overridden by dividing into smaller groups.

Model loving self-care by staying home when you have a drippy nose, moist cough, or fever. One of your gifts to the world should not be your germs. Showing up sick is not heroic; it's inconsiderate.

HEALTHY HELPING

People claiming to get "warm fuzzies" from helping others are apparently telling the literal truth. They're experiencing a feeling Allan Luks, former executive director of the Institute for the Advancement of Health, calls "helper's high."[25]

Luks' research from the late 1980s still holds true: there's a powerful connection between helping others and enhanced health. According to his research, even people with chronic, debilitating diseases such as asthma, arthritis, lupus, and multiple sclerosis report improvements in physical health as a result of helping. People who are depressed perk up considerably.

Helper's high, during which an endorphin rush triggers sensations of physical warmth and increased energy, is the first phase of what Luks identified as the "healthy helping syndrome." During phase two, helpers are able to sustain a more durable sense of calm, relaxation, and equanimity. Luks found that volunteers' self-perception of health and well-being was indisputably tied to the act of helping. Even more fascinating was his finding that warm fuzzies could be restored by simply remembering participation. In addition, the best health results seem to come from regular, frequent, and personal contact with *strangers!*

Eat lunch and take work breaks with those who serve along with you. The benefits of doing this include meeting new people, building community, and getting the scoop on what's really going on.

Commit to upping the delight quotient. When you brought cupcakes for the whole class on your birthday, didn't the day go better? As an adult, you once again have the opportunity to lift everyone's spirit by bringing in treats, whether or not it's your birthday. Extra points for you if you provide something chocolaty *and* salty.

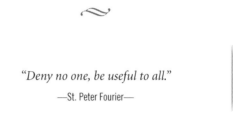

"Deny no one, be useful to all."
—St. Peter Fourier—

Call or text ahead if you know you'll be late. Sometimes in a volunteer service situation, promptness may seem less important when, in fact, it's usually more so. If you tend to run late, set your watch ahead ten to fifteen minutes. If that doesn't work, you probably need to choose a different day or time to show up. If you still can't seem to arrive on time, something else—like resistance—is going on. Maybe you're in the wrong environment entirely.

There's a lot to be said for having a "gut reaction," but some feelings may masquerade as others. Excitement may feel like anxiety, anger may really be fear, and fear may really be hurt. Pay attention to emotions, but don't let them over determine your actions. Serving as an act of will is as valid as jumping into (or out of) something because it "feels" right—at that moment, anyway.[26]

CONTEMPLATIVE WRITING EXERCISE
RESISTING RESISTANCE

One way to prevent self-sabotage is to take an unflinching look at when, how, and why you hold back, slack, or run away. These questions will help you figure out patterns of resistance and avoidance sabotaging your efforts to reach out and grow. Look at your responses. Which attitudes and behaviors are no longer necessary? What can you do right now to enhance your ability to stay committed?

- When do I usually lose interest in activities?
- What tends to turn me off to others?
- How do I typically withdraw from situations or activities?
- What's going on physically, emotionally, and spiritually right before I pull or turn away?
- How does my experience benefit from bailing out?
- What helps me stay conscious and present?

CHAPTER 5

The Shadow Side of Service

INTRODUCTION

You initially planned to manifest the gentle glory of your enlightened presence by serving others with empathy, generosity, and dignity. You, after all, were blessed to receive a call to service you knew was authentic because of the ease with which everything came together. You were led to the perfect place for *doing* as well as *being*, and now you're deep into wondering: "Is it still God's grace if I hate it?"

What happened? This divinely inspired service gig is not the slightest bit illuminating; it's more heart-hardening than opening, and for sure, you're not having fun. Even more distressing is the fact you're barely able to muster any respect for the people you believed would epitomize human decency. Who knew The Cause would be staffed by such self-righteous goobers? As for the cause itself, you're beginning to catch yourself thinking like those you once dismissed as fascists.

Unfortunately, you're also beginning to love watching lots of stupid TV because it takes your mind off nonsense going on in the name of serving others. You're feeling lousy physically, never fully able to shake the dull headache someone had the nerve to suggest might be the body's manifestation of soulless discomfort. In addition, you're so obviously disgruntled that friends and family are beginning to notice—whenever you happen to be around, that is.

Welcome to the shadow side of service! If you thought a heartfelt commitment to serve would be sufficient to ward off the forces of evil, you were wrong. If anything, spiritual types from all traditions agree that nothing quite bugs demons and fallen angels like acts of human kindness. Since service as a form of love in action, you can expect all sorts of disappointments and other darker distractions to emerge as you seek to live life this way.

Whether you actively know it or not, you always have a choice. There are many things you can do to stay focused on what you've been called to do—including finding another place to fulfill your vocation. This, of course, will require entering yet another discernment process which you, the Seeker, are more than willing to do, right? Welcome to the continuous loop of spiritual growth. Meanwhile, you'll need to learn how to deal with the jerks, scoundrels, incompetents, and frauds you encounter along the way. This chapter's tips will help you do that without doing damage to yourself or others.

CHAPTER TIPS

Every six months, make time to reassess what you're doing and where. Turn to a clean page in your journal, and jot down every cause you're championing, plus all activities capturing your time and attention. Not having enough energy to do even this reality check may explain why you're feeling so cranky and tired.

CONTEMPLATIVE WRITING EXERCISE
BOUNDARIES

Boundaries are limits you sent on what you perceive as insensitive or inappropriate behavior coming your way from others. The more firm the boundary, the greater your protection. One danger, of course, is establishing exceedingly rigid boundaries, thus walling yourself in so tightly there's little room for growth. You may become so intent on setting boundaries you end up creating a fortress.

Knowing it's important to establish boundaries does not automatically mean you know what they are or should be. You can better predict sources of discomfort or downright pain by doing some contemplative writing. Use these questions to review how you've handled boundary violations in the past and how you currently respond when things feel out of whack.

It's perfectly okay to squirm as you recall the kid who swiped your monkey puppet in first grade or when your mother threw out your blankie. More intense feelings, such as shame and grief, demand closer attention. It may be time (again?) to explore the meaning and use of personal boundaries with a psychotherapist. Be gentle with yourself as you contemplate:

- How, in the past, did you know someone was stepping over your boundaries?
- These days, how do you know someone is stepping over your boundaries?
- Do you react differently when physical as opposed to emotional boundaries are ignored?
- Are your reactions physical, emotional, or both?
- Which of your protective responses seem to work and which ones do not?

Still not sure what would constitute a healthy boundary? You may be generating your own *tsouris*. Here are boundary-collapsing behaviors for you to swear off:

- Jumping in to fight other people's battles or letting others rush in to fight yours
- Believing you absolutely have to pitch in every time you're asked
- Providing "feedback," no matter how well-intended, without an invitation to do so
- Riffling through someone's desk, files, or pockets without permission

And some no-no's for you to stop coming your way:

- Letting anyone yell, parade, belittle, or mock you and your work
- Allowing yourself to be stuck with, talked into, or shamed into doing extra work or taking on last-minute assignments
- Becoming caught in a continuous loop of doing stuff that didn't work the first dozen times
- Tolerating erratic and contradictory schedule changes, directions, and requests

"*Despair is the absolute extreme of self-love.*"

—Thomas Merton—

Establish a healthy separation between private and public worlds by creating a ritual to mark your entrance into and departure from service situations. This may be as ceremonial as reciting a special prayer before leaving your car or as down-to-earth as putting on and taking off your name tag with consciousness and a sense of purpose.

Prepare to cultivate greater flexibility when it comes to establishing personal boundaries. Legally speaking, you cannot be questioned or badgered about your age, race, gender, marital status, religion, or sexual preference. At the same time, you may find some service environments demand a more intimate level of disclosure about such things, in addition to more openness about feelings and emotions. This seems particularly true of community settings that you should probably avoid if you have strong privacy needs that you have no interest in "working through."

Working hard is not the same thing as struggling. So what's the difference? The sense of fulfillment you experience as a result of working like a pack mule more than makes up for any resulting exhaustion. Exhaustion accompanied by feeling discouraged and powerless indicates struggle. Whether the struggle is worth the hassle depends on what you believe, as well as what you'll tolerate.

Uh-oh, the Executive Director has developed a "thing" for you?!? Be careful. The social standards and legal restrictions regulating intimate conduct in business and academic environments apply to nonprofit service organizations as well. Don't become confused by whatever glow may accompany working shoulder-to-shoulder for a grand cause. Here, as in business, you've every right to say:

- I feel uncomfortable when you make those comments.

- Please respect my wish not to be patted or hugged.

- This is starting to feel like harassment to me.

Maintain zones of personal space by standing no less than two feet away when you're having a work-related conversation. Moving closer may be perceived as intimacy or, depending on content, a threat. Standing too far away may make you seem standoffish. Pay attention to how you're feeling. Discomfort is a clue you feel at risk in some way.

You have every right to say "no" to anything beyond your scope of expertise or comprehension or which is, in your humble opinion, a recipe for disaster. It's *how* you say "no" that will make a difference. Ditch the drama, and simply express what's true for you. Here are some options:

- Thank the person for thinking of you, politely decline, and leave it at that.

- Calmly explain why you're not qualified in this instance, but point out where and how else you could pitch in.

- Graciously propose an alternative person or approach.

Break requests down into manageable parts, agreeing to do some things and declining to do others. Maybe you can drive someone to the Social Security office but cannot provide the ride home. Maybe you can deliver meals to the homebound, but you won't be able to prepare them.

Clarify emotional boundaries by changing the way you articulate *to yourself* reasons for saying "no." The next time you're asked to do something that makes of your entire being recoil, try this: Instead of telling yourself you "can't" do whatever is being asked, shift your thinking to tell yourself how you "won't." Now how do you feel? Stronger? Better? Shifting from "can't" to "won't" should help you distinguish resistance from authentic opposition.

> *"Learn to say no. It will be of more use to you than being able to read Latin."*
> —Charles H. Spurgeon—

In the presence of an impossible request, utter this magic sentence: "Let me get back to you." During your borrowed time, check your motives. What do you think will happen if you decline? Which "yes" responses come from guilt, pride, or ego? Which "no" responses come from fear, defiance, or self-care? Saying "no" may provide just the spiritual opportunity you need, if not want, for more growth. Experiment with saying "no," the letting go completely of whatever might happen next.

Count on running into more than one person who reminds you of someone you can't stand. Never mind if that person is a dead ringer for your ex or waves her hands like the high school soccer coach who benched you. Shift your focus to the person, not the behavioral or physical triggers…if you can.

Sad but true: whatever you cannot stomach in someone else is what you cannot tolerate in yourself. We get to see ourselves in the mirror of relationship. On this point many great philosophers and psychologists agree. Remember this as you stew over someone else's irritating behavior.

Another bit of relational wisdom, this time from third grade, is captured in the retort: "I'm rubber, you're glue. Whatever you say bounces off me and sticks onto *you*." This is worth remembering, but not repeating.

Spiritually speaking, turnabout is *not* fair play. When someone or something else is bugging you, consider making prayer your first, rather than last, resort. Nope, this is not permission to pray, "Dear God, remove this being for my existence." Instead, try praying for the:

- happiness and well-being of the person you can't stand;
- best possible resolution of the situation you find intolerable; and

- ability and willingness to release your intense desire for a specific outcome.

> *"Your enemy is your greatest teacher."*
> —Buddhist saying—

The burning conviction that you absolutely must say or do something before you explode is a strong signal to keep your mouth shut. Unless someone's life is truly at stake, there are a few things that cannot wait at least twenty-four hours before being addressed. Wait until you no longer feel an overwhelming sense of urgency. This goes double for handling situations via email or social media. Click on "delete" instead of "reply" after you read something activating.

YOU WANT ME TO DO *WHAT*???

When you first became active in The Cause, you had some pretty highfalutin dreams about what you'd be called upon to do. Your favorite fantasies involved being asked to make an über-heroic sacrifice. You'd be asked to do something that would call forth your Higher Self. Never in your wildest nightmares did you expect the über-heroic sacrifice would involve anything immoral, or worse, illegal.

Since service comes from light, count on darkness making an appearance sooner or later. Don't be too surprised if, at some point, you find yourself wrestling the demons of deception, falsehood, fakery, secrecy, concealment, entrapment, hypocrisy, stealing, cheating, overindulgence, or greed. You're asked to fudge a few financial figures, keep a secret that demands disclosure, look the other way, or substitute accuracy for truth. Yipes!

It's particularly difficult to win this wrestling match when the request is cleverly presented as your grand opportunity to practice surrender, obedience, and faith. Hopefully, the fact you're spiritually ready to be of service also means you've done enough inner work to sense when something is terribly wrong. If you don't recognize it cognitively, you'll feel it physically or emotionally. Trust your gut and, perhaps, with great disappointment and sadness, move on— with your integrity and soul intact.

"The greater and more valuable the enterprise, the more fatigue and danger you incur: there's no way out of evil except by opposing it."

—St. Angela Merici—

Diffuse another person's attempt to sabotage your contributions by enlisting his or her support in advance. Remember that negativity usually has to do with the other person's lack of ego strength or diminished sense of security. The compassionate phrase, "I'd like to hear what you think about this" will be balm to a pained soul. Fighting back—clean or dirty—will ultimately fail.

If the advanced spiritual practice of seeing God in everyone isn't quite cutting it, try visualizing your perceived opponent as a helpless, diapered baby or an insecure adolescent. But be careful if you resort to this exercise; the point is to feel merciful, not superior! Good luck.

"We must be the change we wish to see in the world."
—Gandhi—

Just because something feels personal doesn't mean it is. You can make yourself nuts by imagining what others do or say is about or because of you. In its extreme form, this behavior is known as paranoia (also evidence of narcissism). Nevertheless, there are situations that, if they persist, are worth checking out, such as being "forgotten" for key meetings or celebratory luncheons. Before confronting anyone with your worst suspicions:

- Write a list of these incidents, and examine them in the light of your own possible hypersensitivity.
- Check your suspicions out with a trusted observer.
- Get honest with yourself about what you want to happen.

Only after doing all this should you take the next step of saying, "Jeepers, this seems like it's getting personal and not in a good way."

At last! Some wants *your* advice or opinion. Watch out! In highly politicized settings, this can be hazardous to your organizational health. First, buy time with this mature response: "Let me think about it and get back to you." Next, consider how your pearls of wisdom might be invoked. One way to test intent is to say, "Thanks for wanting to know what I think. I'd be happy to share my viewpoint at a meeting." Don't be too surprised if your vote suddenly no longer matters. If your offer is accepted, be grateful. You may have misheard, but at least you won't be misquoted.

> *"Ambition is the mother of unhappiness and*
> *prefers to sulk in corners and dark places.*
> *It cannot understand the light of day."*
> —St. Bernard—

Watch out for the sentence "I was only kidding" which, properly translated, means "I meant every word." This verbal backpedaling is akin to teasing and needling. All are attempts to cloak resentment, jealousy, disrespect, fear, and other not-so-grand sentiments under the guise of humor. You could ignore this, harkening back to the "consider the source" lesson you presumably learned during middle school. Or you could firmly and gently respond with one of the following:

- "Gee, it didn't sound like you were kidding."
- "I get the sense there's something you really want to say. It's okay to give it to me directly."
- "Am I doing something that's pushing your buttons? If so, I'd like to hear what it is."

Note: "I was only kidding" is right up there with "Let me be perfectly honest."

Don't agree? Simply say so instead of verbally zapping perceived opponents—or oppressors—with digs and zingers. Instead, try registering your opposition by saying, "I'm afraid I don't agree" or "I probably handle this differently." Offering intelligent, credible reasons for your position will enhance your ability and future right to disagree.

Learn how to communicate anger so it doesn't inappropriately leech, splatter, or gush out on others, by:

- Paying attention to timing, expressing yourself in as close to "real time" as you can *without succumbing to pure emotion.* Better yet, hold off for at least 24 hours.

- Expressing the full, florid expression of your feelings in writing no one but you will ever see. Destroy or delete this document.

- Asking a trusted other to listen to you vent—with or without providing a reality check.

- Taking a stroll around the block—or the neighboring state.

> "You will not be punished for your anger, you will be punished by your anger... Overcome anger by love."
> —Gautama Buddha—

Examine your own "control issues," especially if you generally rebel against anyone in authority. Having to be the alpha puppy is generally an indication that you confuse control with domination and authority with authoritarianism. Hooray! It's time for (more) psychotherapy, especially if the person in charge bears an uncanny resemblance to Mommy or Daddy.

Try embracing this paradox when you feel moved to complain: know what you want changed *and* remain open to the possibility that whatever you don't like is perfectly fine the way it is.

> "God weeps... over a leader who domineers
> over the community."
> —The Talmud—

Feeling overwhelmed is generally a sign you need a dose of solitude. But why wait until you're approaching meltdown? Pull out (or access online!) your calendar, and schedule regular time for relaxation, rest, and reflection. This is important if your service involves interacting with lots of people, critically necessary if you deal with lots of people with lots of problems.

Next time you're feeling bothered and bewildered, opt for becoming curious rather than cheesed off. Examine all

aspects of the situation as you would a marvelous piece of
art or strange bug. Shift from asking God to fix, change, or
remove what or who is irking you to praying for knowledge.

Meeting fire with fire only creates a bigger blaze. Try calibrating
your energy to balance whatever incendiary communications
device is coming at you. In the presence of yelling or screaming,
speak softly and calmly. Answer frenetic questions slowly and
deliberately. Keep your cool when things heat up, responding
to harshness with as much (non-patronizing) gentleness as
you can muster. Remember these forms of verbal abuse almost
always come from those who suffer from fear, unhappiness, or
low self-esteem. It's time (again) to practice empathy.

> *"If you shut the door to all errors,*
> *truth will be shut out."*
> —Tagore—

Physically remove yourself from activating situations until
you get a grip, but don't storm out. If you're the one whose
blood pressure is building, saying something like "I need
some time to calm down" is good way to start the calming
down process. It's a little trickier if someone else is bouncing
off the walls in your direction. Telling someone to "calm down"
or "relax" is almost guaranteed to produce more sound and
fury. It's much more disarming to say, "I think we *both* need

a timeout." And what will *you* be doing during that time out?
Looking at your part by asking:

- What's my contribution to this brouhaha?
- What could I have done differently?
- What do I need to say or do to defuse the situation?

Instead of going numb or rushing to fix everything in the
presence of suffering, consider taking the opposite tack. It may
seem incongruous, but you can better protect yourself from
becoming jaded by acknowledging the range of emotions you
feel—sorrow, judgment, fear, anger, revulsion, compassion.
What you feel is not in and of itself bad or wrong; it's what
you do with these feelings that matters. You'll enhance your
ability to be of service by giving yourself enough time to feel
the enormity of whatever you encounter.

CONTEMPLATIVE WRITING EXERCISE
ILLUMINATING THE SHADOW

Ah, the things that go bump in the darker recesses of
our hearts. If you want to serve with greater authenticity,
it's time to acknowledge attitudes and feelings that might
get in the way. Taking as a given that you're already forgiven
by a loving God, what are you willing to expose to the light
of consciousness? Give yourself permission to finish the
sentences:

I have no tolerance for: _____.

The social problem I can't comprehend is: _____.

I've trouble summoning compassion for: _____.

> *My patience is limited when it comes to:*_____.
>
> *I tend to become extremely frustrated when:* _____.
>
> *I believe human suffering is caused by:*_____.
>
> *Basically, I think most people are:*_____.
>
> *I feeling capable of loving:* _____.
>
> *If I had to choose between my well-being and someone else's, I would choose:* _____.
>
> *Doing this exercise makes me feel:* _____.

> "*Everybody is unique. Compare not yourself with anybody else lest you spoil God's curriculum.*"
> —Baal Shem Tov—

Cultivate an on-site buddy with whom you can share frustrations emerging as you try to be a good, decent, loving human being. Your best buddy bet is someone who winces, twitches, or laughs out loud at the same situations as you. Turn to this kindred spirit for reality checks. Note: Unless you can truly resist the temptation to wisecrack, do not sit together during meetings.

Take a valid verbal nonviolence and swear off:

- griping
- gossiping
- sarcasm
- swearing (out loud, anyway)

Sometimes a gripe cannot go unaddressed. Advance planning will help you complain without sounding like a malcontent. First, take an inventory of what you think isn't working. Next, examine your complaint to clarify your role and responsibility in the matter. Finally, manage your delivery so that you sound significantly less screechy and prepubescent.

You got stuck in traffic, you forgot your lunch, there's a letter from the IRS in the morning mail, and your hair looks lousy. Striving to be a Holy Person, you think this stuff shouldn't matter, but it does and you're in a foul mood. In situations like these, confession is more effective than transcendence. Let everyone know you're cranky, not by acting out, but by saying what's so and asking to be given time and space.

Transform competition into collaboration by appealing to the greater good of all. Yes, some good-natured rivalry (e.g., "Yeah, well, I serve lunches *and* perform CPR") can be motivating, but watch out for any competition generating ill will in the form of someone having to be "better than" or do "more than." You'll almost always be able to generate better results, as well as more dignity and peace, by fostering collaboration (e.g., "I believe we'll accomplish more by sharing our talents, skills, and energy on this project").

Feeling stressed? How about bored? Sullen? You can quickly transform the most dismal mood or surrounding work pit by spritzing a few frequent drops of essential oil onto the floor or into the air. To perk up, use: peppermint, rosemary, grapefruit, light lemon, or eucalyptus. To mellow out, use: orange, sandalwood, or lavender. Combining lavender with peppermint will help you feel pleased about being alert. Note: Essential oils are potent, so get them in little bottles that dispense individual drops. Sniff, do not taste; keep them off your skin and away from heat or flame. If you're in recovery from addiction, look for essential oils without an alcohol base.

SURVIVING SERVICE
THE ULTIMATE PRAYER

Let nothing disturb you,
nothing frighten you.
All things are passing.
God never changes.
Patience obtains all things.
Nothing is wanting to him
who possesses God.
God alone suffices.

–St. Teresa of Avila

Sometimes good causes attract bad people. It's okay to notice this; just don't squander precious energy getting riled up about reality. Instead, put your energy toward staying on the side of the angels.

CONTEMPLATIVE WRITING EXERCISE
WHY MOI?

Mama said there'd be days like this: Why on earth did you ever agree to help anyone do anything? This stinketh. What were you thinking?

Well, if you've been on the spiritual path for a while, you probably thought some nifty inner growth was available. You're just having a wee bit of trouble perceiving and appreciating what that growth might be. Writing out your responses to these questions after a tough day of doing good will help lead you back to the heart of service:

- What did I learn today?
- How did I help?
- When was I most present to what was happening?
- How is my life being enhanced?

Do not underestimate the stress of being around a lot of noise from people, equipment, traffic, and natural disasters. The best antidote to noise is silence. Make sure you eliminate or at least significantly reduce all aural stimulation as soon as you can. Listen to soothing music on your way home. Once there, render all electronic equipment inaudible for at least an hour. Let your housemate, partner, spouse, kid(s), or pets know you need a period of silent downtime to calm body, soul, and spirit after tough day of giving.

DEALING WITH CAREGIVER STRESS

You've taken on the role of primary caregiver for a loved one who is sick, aging poorly, or in the process of dying. Your brother lives on another planet, your younger sister makes everyone crazy, and the aunties have their own *mishagas*. Tag. You're it!

Fortunately, you believe serving this way is morally right. Still, the buffer of self-righteousness can wear pretty thin after a spell of dealing with managed healthcare providers, feeding tubes, and adult diapering. Also, you can start to experience a slow, steady decline in your own health. It's not at all unusual for strong feelings and emotions such as anger, grief, and overwhelming frustration to show up as high blood pressure, stomachaches, dizziness, acid reflux, blurred vision, headaches, generalized muscle soreness, sleeplessness, and exhaustion.

Discounting the symptoms, or ignoring them altogether, can lead to even more horrifying disorders and diseases such as arteriosclerosis, heart attack, stroke, migraine, eating disorders, fibromyalgia, or chronic fatigue immune deficiency syndrome.

You can prevent stress by taking an increasingly significant toll on your health by getting:

- psychological support for feelings and emotions from a therapist or support group;
- aches and pains treated before they turn into something more serious;
- enough regular sleep, meals, exercise, and contact with friends;
- instruction in relaxation techniques such as meditation, visualization, biofeedback, and *hatha yoga*.

Treat yourself to extreme self-care by going way beyond minimal daily requirements to keep body and soul together.

Don't wait for someone's permission to nurture yourself or
an unexpected gift certificate to a day spa. Take the initiative
to add naps, warm baths, and food treats to your regular
regimen. Set aside time to read poetry, say prayers, or do
absolutely nothing but stare at your floating eye motes. Note:
Think carefully about continuing to serve in an environment
that does not recognize these very human needs.

SPIRITUAL ABUSE? WELL, IF IT QUACKS LIKE A DUCK...

Trusting soul that you are, you figured becoming part
of the spiritual community would do nothing but enhance
your ability and willingness to serve others. Maybe. Maybe
not. Entering a community, even one with a venerated religious tradition of service does not guarantee you'll become
a living embodiment of the St. Francis prayer. Indeed, you
may find quite the opposite happens.

Instead of feeling uplifted and ever more clear about
your vocation, you find yourself feeling put upon, confused,
and, yes, abused. Do not let transcendental smells and bells
obscure reality. In all likelihood, feeling violated means
that's exactly what's going on. Still not sure? Here's a handy
checklist of transgressions commonly found in spiritual
communities:[27]

- Turns out the community is not speaking metaphori-
  cally when referring to itself as a family. Those in charge
  are just like Mother and Father or both. You may even
  be instructed to refer to them as such. You get to be the
  child, returning not to a state of innocence and wonder,
  but one of helplessness and blind obedience.
- Serving others requires giving up all worldly goods for
  the glory of God, but you notice spiritual leadership
  lives pretty high on the hog.
- You're required to handle basic survival needs on a
  schedule that's downright odd, not to mention massively

inconvenient (i.e., three-minute showers on Wednesdays at 4 a.m.).

- Community "elders" seem capricious, arbitrary, or just simply wacko. These folks have the power to make your life a living hell and will do so with relatively little provocation.
- Anyone who does not share the exact same *expression* of beliefs is judged as wrong or bad, possibly demonically possessed. There's no open, safe, community-wide forum to discuss thoughts, feelings, or beliefs.
- Rules and rituals for community life make no sense and cannot be relegated to the domain of Mystery. Messing up or refusing to participate in special ways of walking, kneeling, sitting, speaking, not speaking, eating, fasting, sleeping, or thinking is grounds for punishment.
- Attempts to "modify" your attitudes or behaviors are justified by such spiritualized explanations as: "God told me..." or "I'm led to tell you..." or "According to Scripture..." or "The Guru said..."
- Punishment, sometimes referred to as discipline or education, involves ostracism, community-wide humiliation, a period of isolation, or being relegated to demeaning and unnecessarily precise chores like making sure all window shades in the entire building are at exactly the same height.
- You start to lose or gain weight; can't sleep at all or want to sleep all the time; have unexplained crying or laughing jags; become extremely short-tempered or laissez-faire to a fault. Being of service to others has gone from dream to waking nightmare.

"The soul is a guest in our body,
deserving of our kind hospitality."
—Hillel—

An organization's needs may be at odds with your own desire to change and grow. Create a mechanism for knowing or evaluating when it's time to move on or to do something different. This may take the form of a five-point scale or a simple ten-point checklist of items you want to accomplish. Revisit this twice, at three-month intervals, and then either reevaluate your expectations, accept the way it is, or leave.

> *"The angels are here, they are at your side, they are with you, present on your behalf."*
> —St. Bernard of Clairvaux—

Be prepared to head for the door if what the organization professes to be doing is not, in fact, what it *is* doing. But before deciding to leave, make every effort to:

- Check, through prayer, meditation, and discussion with a trusted other, whether you're being overly critical, judgmental, or reactive.

- Voice concerns in a way others can hear, then allow time for change to happen.

- Be equally willing to act on what you believe and to have a change of heart.

"A person who says 'I'm enlightened'
probably isn't."

—Ram Dass—

CONTEMPLATIVE WRITING EXERCISE
RETURNING TO CENTER

Now you're really confused. What you thought was true is false. What you believed was right is wrong. What you hoped was light is dark. It's time to return to center by doing a bit of contemplative writing in response to these questions:

- What did I feel initially called to do?
- In what ways has my participation answered that calling?
- How, if at all, has my calling changed?
- What am I now call to do or be?
- Where am I now call to serve?

Service Is Its Own Reward

To tell the truth, my most recent foray into service was significantly less uplifting. It was emotionally upsetting and spiritually challenging. I felt like a failure on all levels, which is not exactly my idea of fulfillment. Adding to my upset was the it's-no-coincidence fact that I had pretty much completed writing this book. How humbling, distressing, and flat-out annoying to find myself writing about the value of service while muttering "never again" to no one in particular.

But even as I groused, and even as I write this, I know full well I will answer the call to service again. And again. Why? Because I know what becomes possible whenever I do. This past weekend, in fact, I caught myself feeling so passionate about a social outreach issue that I put my name on a list to serve on a committee of like-minded others. I can't stand committees. Maybe it's time for me to grow past whatever apprehensions underlie that particular stance. Maybe serving solo is stunting my emotional development and spiritual growth.

All this is to say, once you choose a place to serve and get going, watch and watch out! Your life is about to change inside and out, like mine has time and time again. Whatever you once believed about yourself and others will deepen, disappear, and reemerge transformed. Here are a few closing thoughts about service as a spiritual practice.

Plan to see yourself in ways that won't always be pleasing. Just when you think you've attained more than a modicum of serenity, you'll get to see your impatience. You'll feel peeved that whatever you're doing seems utterly thankless and then you'll feel even more peeved that you want to be thanked. Try to observe the flow of feelings and have them. Before too long, you'll discover a generosity of spirit you never knew you had. You'll find thanks for the grace of God, which will show up in unanticipated ways.

Plan to lose faith if you had it and to find faith again after paradise seems irretrievably lost. Just when other people are bugging the living daylights out of you, you'll be granted a moment (possibly longer) of truly knowing God is speaking directly to you through them. All you have to do is listen, which, in itself, is a powerful spiritual practice.

External realities will also shift after you've been engaged in service for a while. Some of the shifts will have more to do with life cycle changes than anything else. Years ago, I'd happily march up and down Manhattan's Avenue of the Americas to make the point about equal rights. Now I'd much rather send money—or an energetic surrogate protester. March the marches while you still want to!

Plan to face the mighty challenge of energy conservation. Wholehearted service will leave you feeling tired and wired. Sometimes grief stricken. Sooner or later, you'll have to decide what to set aside to have more time and energy for the service activities you've come to love. After a while, you find yourself wondering what service work to ditch so you have more time and energy for yourself. My prayer is that you learn how to achieve this balance more easily than I ever have.

Last year, the combined intensity of two service situations led me to the brink of total body, mind, and spirit exhaustion, which I ignored until a nasty sprain forced me to slow down. As I sat at the bottom of the short flight of stairs, squeezing my swiftly ballooning ankle, I laughed out loud with delight (rather than hysteria) for this Divine providence. I said a quick prayer of thanksgiving and then went home to rest with an ice pack on my ankle and two cats on my lap. Thirty-six hours on crutches were enough to persuade me that a serious timeout was the next right thing to do. And once I got out of the way, everyone else had enough room to show up and pitch in, giving me plenty of time for some much-needed contemplative writing of my own.

Plan on receiving some flak from well-meaning friends who may be appalled by what you're willing to do in the name of service. In 1993, I helped care for a friend dying of AIDS. His initial care team was well populated, and because of my faith and high tolerance of gruesome smells and sights, we decided to save me for the final months. By the time he died, the once-massive care team was down to five people. The last weekend he was alive, we communicated primarily through sign language. The "witness consciousness" I had to call forth was unlike anything I'd previously managed to muster. Ever since then, I've willingly volunteered to serve on hospice teams. It doesn't matter that serving this way both lifts my soul and knocks me out; I am always awed by the privilege of being with someone dying.

Like other spiritual practices, service offers a way to confront and heal our own brokenness. I believe (and hope) that by the time you're able to hear and answer the call to service, you've done a fair amount of psychospiritual work. This, alas, is no cause for smug celebration because greater awareness always gives rise to more subtle methods of avoidance.

Last night, for example, having made peace with my decision to take a break from active caregiving, I ignored some of my own best advice and ate three pieces of gefilte fish with beet horseradish; a head of steam to broccoli with extra virgin olive oil and liberal amounts of kosher salt; a smallish bowl of leftover sausage and peppers; and one-third gallon of dairy-free ice cream substitute with walnuts and chocolate syrup. This temporary respite from feeling was good for about three pounds of morning bloat. I took a diuretic and spent most of the day pondering emotions I had been trying to avoid—grief, relief, gratitude, disappointment. Ah yes, now I remember! It's time, once again, to pray for the knowledge of God's will. And I also remember this; as ever, prayer will lead me back onto the path of service. My spiritual journey will continue. Perhaps we'll meet along the way.

— JUNE, 2001

Notes

1   Shameless Self-Promotion Alert: Decades later I would write about how empathy, in and of itself, could be a powerful spiritual practice in *Desperately Seeking Spirituality: A Field Guide to Practice* (Collegeville, MN: Liturgical Press, 2016). In addition to empathy, I identify four additional key "practices of being": willingness, curiosity, generosity, and delight.

2   Rereading this Foreword more than a decade later, I'm realizing how the seeds of every book I write really are sown in a previous book. I wrote *Deliberate Acts of Kindness* after writing *Staying Sober: Tips for Working a Twelve Step Program of Recovery* (Center City, MN: Hazelden, 1999). More specifically, a cozy lunch with Howard Maher, of blessed memory, inspired me to spend more time writing about an essential component of Step 12 (Alcoholics Anonymous version): "having had a spiritual awakening as a result of these steps, we tried to carry this message to alcoholics, and to practice these principles in all our affairs."

3   Just a few of what are known as the corporal and spiritual works of mercy, Gospel imperatives neatly organized by St. Thomas Aquinas. Full list of works of material and physical generosity: feed the hungry; shelter the homeless; clothe the naked; visit the sick and imprisoned; bury the dead; give alms to the poor.

4   Conversations about being "spiritual but not religious" began emerging in 2001 with Robert C. Fuller's book, *Spiritual, but Not Religious: Understanding Unchurched America* (New York: Oxford University press, 2001). Books, articles, blog posts both snarky and nice about SBNRs (Spiritual but Not Religious) were especially abundant for the following decade or so. In 2015, observers of this scene welcomed Kaya Oakes' book, *The Nones Are Alright* (Maryknoll, NY: Orbis Books, 2015) which overlapped with pieces about "spiritual refugees" known as the "Dones." See Mark Sandlin, "The Rise of the Dones As the Church Kills Spiritual Community," *The God Article* (Patheos Progressive), November 21, 2014: http://bit.ly/2aA0nzU and Joshua Packard, "Meet the 'Dones,'" *Leadership Journal* (*Christianity Today*), Summer 2015: http://bit.ly/2azZJCF.

5   Judaism has "movements" rather than denominations. Primary ones: Orthodox, Conservative, Reform, and Reconstructionist. As is the case with Christian denominations, you'll find distinctions within movements (e.g., Ultra-Orthodox, Modern Orthodox) and debates about who is doing any of it as God intended.

6   Scripture verses too numerous to cite, even with the assistance of the handy-dandy website, BibleGateway: http://www.biblegateway.com.

7   "Joint Declaration on the Doctrine of Justification by the Lutheran World Federation and the Catholic Church," October 31, 1999: http://bit.ly/2acRKIh. If you don't want to plow through that, read this review and analysis: John Bookser Feister, "Faith and Works: Catholics and Lutherans Find Agreement," in *St. Anthony Messenger* (AmericanCatholic.org), June 2000: http://bit.ly/2acSGfB. For an example from those eternally opposed, read: Paul T. McCain, "A Betrayal of the Gospel: the Joint Declaration on The Doctrine of Justification," *First Things,* March 12, 2010: http://bit.ly/2aAb7hw. Go ahead—take a WAG when I think about this brouhaha. Don't know what "WAG" means? Google it.

8   For a contemporary take on the Rule, see: John McQuiston, *Always We Begin Again: The Benedictine Way of Living* (Harrisburg, PA: Morehouse Publishing, 1996).

9   I want those of you who are reading these endnotes (added to this second edition) to know Louise was the name of one of my cats while I was writing this book—and a few others. She was a wonderful, happy calico. The other cat, the one with tabbitude, was (a tabby) named Thelma, of course!

10   Another great example of which seeds get sown where! Until I worked on the second edition, I'd forgotten just how long I've been interested in when and how the venerable spiritual practices stop working for longtime Seekers. Fifteen years after writing and publishing this book, I'd explore those issues in *Desperately Seeking Spirituality: A Field Guide to Practice* (Collegeville, MN: Liturgical Press, 2016). [Muttering to self: at least you are consistent somewhere.]

11   Take a look at this eleven-second video featuring a trust fall. Trust me, you won't be disappointed: http://bit.ly/2aAgJJ0.

12   For years during the 1980s and 1990s, I'd be jolted awake at 3:00 a.m. with insights. I wrote them down on notecards, and then filed and forgot about them. Years later, during a cleaning fit, I found those notecards and was awed (in the true sense of the word) not only by what had been revealed to me years earlier but what had come to pass.

13 A classic and readable text about such groups—their formation and process: Suzanne G. Farnham, Joseph P. Gill, R. Taylor McLean, and Susan M. Ward, *Listening Hearts: Discerning Call in Community,* Second Edition with Expanded Guidelines for Discernment (Harrisburg, PA: Morehouse Publishing, 1991).

14 No shortage of books about the Examen created by St. Ignatius Loyola, and here's my favorite among them: Jim Manney, *A Simple, Life-Changing Prayer: Discovering the Power of St. Ignatius Loyola's Examen* (Chicago, IL: Loyola Press, 2011).

15 Yet another classic: Ken Dychtwald, *BodyMind* (New York: Jeremy P. Tarcher/Penguin, 1977, 1986).

16 By the end of the 1990s I, for one, was more than happy to fold blankets and prep enough Brussels sprouts to serve 450 people. Not so during the 1970s when I stormed off to see the monk-in-charge at an ashram after noticing how all the "guru brothers" got to chant the bazillion names of God while all the "guru sisters" were stuck peeling and chopping onions. And this was *before* my feminist awakening.

17 While writing *Desperately Seeking Spirituality* I learned that R & R makes more sense when articulated as "relaxation and rest" rather than the other way around. For more about why plus suggestions about how to accomplish both R's, please read that book!

18 Not to brag (much), but I once scored a hospital bed by calling the purchasing agent of a local hospital and asking if they had any beds they wanted to get rid of—they did.

19 I rarely, if ever, pass up an opportunity to mention that I'm a sociologist by education and training. I also hasten to explain that this means I have an advanced degree in noticing what people are doing; observing how they behave, especially in groups; sorting them into categories; and making evidence-based generalizations that usually annoy people without any social science education or training. I love being a sociologist!

20 One major exception is serving within the world of church where everything is exacerbated by the assumption that people will be better, nicer, and kinder in that environment. Not a great assumption to make, an assertion I feel comfy stating after nearly two decades of paid and volunteer church work as staff as well as a consultant. I routinely advise people to examine how they do and will sustain their faith while working for the institutional church.

21   I believe this is even more important now than when I first wrote it because so much has changed nationally in the United States of America as well as internationally since 2001. As a matter of factoid, I'm writing this footnote at a time when a lack of knowledge about the history of women as well as racial, ethnic, and religious minorities is particularly evident and deeply troubling. That's right; I'm writing this in July 2016.

22   This would be a good place to note that guilt and shame are not the same feelings, at least not to clinicians and anyone involved with serious self-examination. So what's the distinction? Guilt is feeling badly about something you've done. Shame is feeling badly about who you are. Big difference. I also feel compelled to add that I've come to believe guilt has become a highly underrated emotion, but that might be because I was raised Jewish, received Confirmation in the Roman Catholic Church, and am well beyond (chronological) middle age.

23   I have never been able (and have pretty much given up trying) to get custody over my facial expressions. Even when I'm chatting online via social media, people seem to know when I'm rolling my eyes. Gift? Curse? At this point, what does it matter? For me. You, however, might want to conquer your personality tics as a manifest in body language. Or not.

24   For those of you keeping score at home, note that some version of this has shown up in just about every book I've ever written. A couple of years ago, someone on Twitter during an online chat tried to convince me that all theories and research about learning styles were bogus. I think they're useful, but if you want to explore why some psychologists challenge the validity and use, check out: Derek Bruff, "Learning Styles: Fact and Fiction – A Conference Report" *Vanderbilt University–The Center for Teaching*, January 28, 2011: http://bit.ly/2aALdug; "Learning Styles Debunked: There Is No Evidence Supporting Auditory and Visual Learning, Psychologists Say," *Association for Psychological Science*, December 16, 2009: http://bit.ly/2adv62f. For an overview of opinions, see: Todd Finley, "Are Learning Styles Real – and Useful?" *Edutopia*, September 22, 2015: http://edut.to/2advxK2.

25   Allan Luks, *The Healing Power of Doing Good* (New York: Ballantine Books, 1991).

26   Rant Alert: When, pray tell, did feeling eclipse thinking? I've lost count—actually, I don't have the stomach to count—how often I hear and read assertions that begin with, "I feel that…" prefatory to articulating something that has everything to do with information/knowledge/thinking. As I write this, I feel

that you might want an example. Here's an example: "I'm feeling that traffic will be busy at that time of day." What *is* that?

27   Happy/sorry to say I've experienced or witnessed everything on this list.

Index

Almsgiving   52
Angels   xiii, 2, 23, 28,
                            74, 92, 95
Benedict of Nursia   7
Bible   1, 2
  Passages:
    2 Corinthians   7
    Deuteronomy   2-3
    Genesis   2-3
    James   6-7
    Leviticus   2-3, 5, 51
    Matthew   6
  People:
    Abraham   2
    Isaac   2
    Israelites   2-3
    Jesus   5-6
    Moses   2
    Paul   7
    Sarah   2
  God or Divine:
    in general   x, xii, xiii
    In Bible   2-3, 6
    Grace of   7, 73, 100
    God's will   8, 20-24, 28,
                             32, 47, 68,
                                73, 95
    Praying to   17, 39, 80,
                              86-87, 91
    Qualities of   82, 86, 88-89
    questioning existence of   13, 52
    seeking God   14, 102
    service   46, 64, 94
Greatest Commandment   5-6
Gospel   6

Prophets   1
Board of Directors   48-50
  Charity (organizations)   33, 54, 62
  Nonprofit   44-45, 48, 78
Boundaries   59, 64, 75-90
Buddhism   8-11, 81
  Bodhisattva   9-10
  Enlightenment   8-9
  Full Realization   8
  Gautama Buddha   85
  Mahayana   9-10
  Nirvana   8-10
  Reincarnation   9
  Theravada   9-10
Call to Service   xiii, xiv, 11,
                            13-29, 31-32,
                             58, 97, 99,
                              101-102
Caregiving   65-66, 70
  Healthy helping syndrome   70-71
  Helper's High   70-71
  Self-sabotage   72
  Stress   92, 93
Catholics   7
Charity (acts of)   9-10, 52,
                              54-55
Christianity   5- 9, 51-52
Communication   58, 69-70,
                              85, 87
  Behavior   15, 22,
                            62-63, 67-68,
                             72, 75-76,
                               80, 83,
                             90-91, 95
Body Language   67

Collaboration	70, 90-91	Talmud	3, 20, 86
Competition	90	Tzedakah	2-6, 52
Intuition	5, 14, 20, 28,	Judeo-Christian	9
	72, 82	Judgment	xiii, 52, 67-68,
Non-verbal	67-68, 72		88, 96
Compassion	xi, xiii, 2, 5-7,	Luther, Martin	7
	9-10, 22, 44,	Meditation	9-11, 13, 31, 93
	63, 66-67, 74,	Merit	9-10
	76, 82, 85, 88	Metta	10-11
Contemplative		Monasticism	7, 27
In general	28, 62, 101	Mosaic Law	6
Writing Exercises for	4-7, 10, 24,	Moses Maimonides	2, 4-5
	28, 36, 42, 66,	Muslim	
	72, 75, 88,	Almsgiving (Sadaqah)	52
	92, 97	Qu'ran	52
Discernment	13-29, 36-37,	Prayer	8, 17-19, 39, 52,
	74, 92, 97		60, 63, 68, 77,
Donate	40-41, 54-55		80, 91, 93-94,
Charity (acts of)	9-10, 52,		96, 101-102
	54-55	Merton, Thomas	39
Goods/items	53	Prayer of St. Francis of Assisi	63
Money	3, 24, 31, 33,	Rossetti, Christina	19
	43, 48, 50-53,	St. Teresa of Avila	91
	100	Protestant Reformation	7
Recycling	40-41, 53	Psychology	19, 67-68, 75,
Dreams	21, 25, 31,		80, 86, 93, 102
	81, 95	Quotes	
Forgiveness	66, 88-89	Baal Shem Tov	64, 89
Golden Rule	6, 9, 24, 42	Buddha, Gautama	85
Heaven and Hell	3, 4, 6, 43,	Dalai Lama	27
	54, 65	Dass, Ram	96
Hierarchy of Needs	16-17	Gandhi	83
Hinduism	8-9	Hillel	94
Intuition	5, 14, 20, 28,	Ignatius of Loyola	25
	72, 82	Maslow, Abraham	16-17
Islam		Mead, Margaret	37
Almsgiving (Zakat)	52	Merton, Thomas	39, 76
Prayer (Salat)	52	Mother Teresa	32
Qu'ran	52	Rabbi Gamaliel	28
Judaism	2-6, 52	Rossetti, Christina	19
Gan Eden	3-4	Spurgeon, Charles H.	79
Gehinnom	3-4	St. Angela Merici	82
Halakhah	2	St. Augustine	15
Jewish Law	xii, 2-6	St. Benedict of Nursia	7-8
Mitzvot	2-4	St. Bernard	84

St. Bernard of Clairvaux   95
St. Francis DeSales   46
St. Francis of Assisi   63
St. John Damascene   24
St. John of the Cross   24
St. Leo the Great   51
St. Peter Fourier   71
St. Teresa of Avila   91
St. Vincent de Paul   62
Tagore   25, 87
Thich Nhat Hanh   67
Upanishads   69
Wesley, John   x, 60
Retreats   xii, 45-46,
                               48-49
Righteousness   1-4, 6-7, 23,
                               73, 93
Rule of St. Benedict   7-8, 63
Scripture
  2 Corinthians   7
  Deuteronomy   2-3
  Genesis   2-3
  James   6-7
  Leviticus   2-3, 5, 51
  Matthew   6
Salvation   1, 6-7, 40, 53
Self-actualization   16-17
Self-sabotage   72, 82
Seva   xii, 9
Spiritual Abuse   94-95
Stewardship   52, 54
Suffering   7, 9-10, 14,
                              16, 35, 87-89
Talmud   3, 20, 86
Tithing   2, 6, 51-52
Volunteer   xiv, 26-27, 32-33,
                              35, 38, 41, 43-45, 49,
                              58-62, 70-71, 101
  Volunteer vacation   45-46
Wesley, John   x, 60
World Religions   1-2
  Buddhism   8-11, 81, 85
  Catholicism   7
  Christianity   5-9, 51-52
  Eastern Traditions   8

Hinduism   8-9
Islam   52
Judaism   2-6, 52
Judeo-Christian   9

SCRIPTURES
2 Corinthians 12:9   7
Deuteronomy 26: 12-13   3
Genesis 1:26   3
Genesis 18   2
Genesis 21:1-22:18   2
James 2:14-18   7
Leviticus 27:30-33   3
Matthew 22:37-38   6

PRAYERS
Discerning Service:
  The Ultimate Prayer
  (Christina Rossetti)   19
Starting Service:
  The Ultimate Prayer
  (Thomas Merton)   39
Selfless Service:
  The Ultimate Prayer
  (St. Francis of Assisi)   63
Surviving Service:
  The Ultimate Prayer
  (St. Teresa of Avila)   91

About the Author

Meredith Gould, PhD is a sociologist and longtime spiritual seeker whose work illuminates the spirituality of everyday life. She's an award-winning author of ten books with "always one in the works." Meredith actively engages in conversation and community on Twitter (@meredithgould) and Facebook. Her writing about writing is posted to Medium.

Visit: www.meredithgould for more information about her work and to book speaking engagements.

Made in the USA
Columbia, SC
27 August 2017